P9-CDG-827

In the Beginning
There Were the Parents

In the Beginning
There Were the Parents

Dolores Curran

Winston Press

Copyright © 1978 by Dolores Curran
Library of Congress Catalog Number: 77-91624
ISBN: 0-03-042766-5
Printed in the United States of America

All rights reserved. No part of this book may be reproduced
in any form by any means without written permission from
Winston Press, Inc.

Cover illustration by Richard Brown.

Winston Press, 430 Oak Grove, Minneapolis, MN 55403

Acknowledgments

"Go Get My Wallet" originally appeared in *Marriage Magazine*, published by Abbey Press, St. Meinrad, Indiana 47577.

"Where Are the Catholic Fathers?", "Read It Again, Mom," and "Television—Our Electronic Hearth?" originally appeared in *St. Anthony Messenger*, 1615 Republic St., Cincinnati, Ohio 45210.

Selections were taken from "Talks to Parents," a weekly column by Dolores Curran, syndicated by Alt-Curran Associates, 300 Dauphin St., Green Bay, Wisconsin 54301.

Dedicated to Frank and Winifred Curran

Contents

Introduction

It's been more than seven years since the publication of my first book, *Who, Me Teach My Child Religion?* In that book I gave an autobiographical account of the attitudes, practices, and religious values we were trying to instill within our own family, and I shared some of our ways for doing that. Back then, the idea of involving Catholic parents in the religious education of their children was considered radical. Friends told me I was wasting my time by writing for parents and that I'd be better off writing religious textbooks.

I'm happy to say they were wrong. Since 1970, parent education and family-centered religious education have come of age in our Church. I've addressed dozens of major religious education congresses on some phase of *Family*. Major religious documents now emanating from Rome, our bishops, and diocesan offices speak of the prime importance of educating the parents. In 1976 the bishops held a Call to Action consultation, which drew more response to *Family* than to any other issue except *Church*. Most dioceses now have a department dedicated solely to enriching the family. My monthly column, "Talks to Parents," now goes into two million homes via diocesan papers, newsletters, and parish bulletins.

During these past seven years, I have met with and heard from thousands of Catholic parents—the very ones designated earlier as those who "just won't get interested." These parents *are* interested in a family life made richer and stronger through faith. They want help in furnishing a warm religious environment in the home. But they also want help in parenting in general. They keep hearing that the family is in trouble, but they don't act as if they believe it, because they keep trying to improve family life by reading, learning, praying, attending workshops, and sharing with one another.

A noticeable difference in parents today compared to parents at the time I wrote *Who, Me?* is their wider view of religion. In 1968-69 parents were terribly concerned about doctrine. Now they want to know how to help members of their families communicate better, how to handle pressures affecting family life—television, permissiveness, drugs—, how to enrich their marriages, and how to teach members of their families compassion and responsibility for others. In short, they want religion to be something they can apply to the everyday lived experience of the family, not just something they can learn.

Who, Me? was a personal book in which I talked about myself and my husband and our children. This is a less personal book but one that is, I hope, no less helpful. My activities in family-centered education have so broadened in scope that I feel I must go beyond discussion of "my children" in this book.

I realize, however, that many of you are interested in my children. You ask me in Seattle, Los Angeles, St. Petersburg, "How old is Beth now?" So, to catch you up, the four-year-old I wrote about is now an energetic teenager, occupied with high school, sports, band, and the eternal telephone. Mike is twelve, and Steve, the youngest, is nine.

Life changes as they age (and I remain ageless), but I disagree with parents who say it changes for the worse. I was amused at the number who wrote after reading *Who, Me?* to say, "Well, maybe you can make these things work for you now, but just wait till your children get to be teenagers." I must admit we have our downs and ups, our battles and reconciliations, our moments of lunacy and intimacy. Sometimes the hormones get hopping so erratically that we wonder why we ever wished our children out of diapers.

But the refreshing and delicious moments of sharing with emerging young adults, who are full of optimism and enthusiasm, make it far more exciting than the first tooth. I may change my assessment before the youngest is out of school, but right now I wouldn't trade these emerging years for the nurturing ones.

I'm grateful to all of you who share in this book, parents who have written or spoken to me, who attest to the great source of strength we have sitting out there in the pew. My thanks, too, to the coordinators and directors of religious education who have not lost the vision of family-centered education—particularly the nuns, who at times have had to battle parents and pastors alike to make them realize that family religion is more than just driving children to religion class.

Special thanks go to my husband Jim and my children, for allowing themselves to be shared with my readers, and to my typist, Editha Quaintance, who has remarkable skill in transforming scratchy rough drafts into neat, orderly lines.

CHAPTER 1

In the Beginning

IN THE BEGINNING there were the parents. They listened to the word and brought it home, where it shone forth at table, in the fields, and before the hearth. They spread the Good News from generation to generation as easily as they planted and harvested the seed.

They were a simple people, these ancestors of ours who tilled the land in Germany, tended the vineyards in Italy, and gathered the potatoes in Ireland. They never studied a catechism, built a school, or heard of CCD. Yet they had a deep abiding Catholic faith. How could that be?

They lived their faith daily. They told time by the convent bells and bowed their heads in prayer at Angelus, wherever they were. Their whole village fasted in Lent and feasted on holy days. They married each other. For most, their whole world lay within their village, and that world went unchanged for centuries. Life was harsh, but faith was easy to pass on.

Then they crossed the ocean to the land of opportunity, America, and they were bewildered. New and alien forces attacked the family structure. The children began asking why they were different, and, faced with the fear of losing their children to this strange new culture, the parents turned to their Church.

They sought and received leadership from the pastor, the parish father. He advised them on many matters, from voter registration to preserving the faith of their children. Out of this leadership the Catholic schools were born.

IN THE MIDDLE there were the *Theys*—nuns, priests, schools. The parents relaxed. Parents concentrated on furnishing a better life for their families and left the job of religion to the *Theys*. *They* would teach the commandments. *They* would teach the children their prayers. *They* would baptize the children, run the schools, and preserve the faith of generations. And *They* did a magnificent job.

So the parents began doing less. No longer did they pray together as a family or sing together the old German hymns. When the school began to send the children to First Communion as a class, the family stopped celebrating it as a family milestone. When the school began teaching units on the saints, the family stopped having special nameday festivities. Hundreds of ethnic customs were lost. Religious storytelling in the home became obsolete.

Eventually the parents forgot how to pass on the Word to their children. They forgot how to pray together as a family. They became embarrassed to sing together. They could no longer talk about God or religion comfortably.

So they blamed the *Theys*. Why weren't *They* teaching their children to pray, to believe, to accept, just as *They* had always done before? And the *Theys*—the priests, nuns, and directors of religious education—explained that *They* were no longer able to do it alone. Teaching religion in the classroom wasn't enough. To be lived, religion had to return to the family.

IN THE END there is the beginning, the Christian family. We are the parents, the beginning and the end of this saga. How we let Christ's words shine forth again at table and in front of the TV set in our Future Shock culture will largely determine our children's present and future faith.

That is what this book is all about—the return to our rightful place as the first and foremost religious educators. Reeducating ourselves to become primary educators is a challenge, especially at this time in history. Life is easier, but faith is harder to pass on. Nevertheless, faith is still worth passing on, and our children still deserve to receive it. So let's make the commitment to them and begin.

Getting It All Together in the Parish

One time I spoke with parents in a parish and encouraged them to take on the religious nourishment of their children. Before I began, the pastor confided in me, "Don't get your hopes too high. These parents just aren't that interested in doing anything themselves."

Later, after the talk, some parents confided in me, "We'd really like to get some small groups together for family religious education, but our pastor isn't interested."

I call this the "Parents-don't-care/Father's-too-busy" syndrome. As long as one of us can use the other as an excuse for inaction, we will continue our inaction.

Exactly what is family religious education? That depends on where you live. In a Denver parish, the whole family attends class on the same night, and all study the same subject. Only the level of teaching changes. The idea is that the family can then go home and discuss that particular facet of their faith with one another during the week.

In Phoenix, small groups of families cluster and teach one another's children and themselves at home. In Minneapolis, parents attend religious-education classes to learn how to teach their children religion, and then they go home and do it.

In some Air Force parishes, the chaplains teach the parents, the parents teach their teenagers, and the teenagers teach the younger children. Hundreds of other parishes hold weekly CCD classes for children with a companion enrichment program for parents. This format is particularly popular for sacramental preparation.

Wherever we are, we can be sure our Director of Education (DRE) is waiting for us to step forward and become our children's primary religion teacher. At the same time, we may be sitting back waiting to be asked. Or we may be actively resisting the invitation, wondering aloud, "Why can't *They* do it? That's what *They* were hired to do."

Even when pastors and DREs have the time to teach weekly classes, they hesitate to do so because it prolongs the idea in parents that "Father can do it better." And it reinforces the idea in children that religion is a subject to be learned, not a life to be lived. It is like math or piano lessons—we study them with some qualified teacher when we're young, but we don't bother about them any more when we grow up. We have enough knowledge for life.

The *General Catechetical Directory* developed in 1971 clearly points out the fallacy of this kind of thinking, which has captured the minds of parents for generations. It emphasizes that teaching adults and parents should be our first objective. Cardinal John Krol, former president of our American bishops, put it more bluntly when he said that the faith of the majority of American Catholics is at "a stunted or adolescent level."

I hear parents say, "I don't know enough to teach my children religion." That's the purpose of the parish, of the DRE, of the pastor: to teach us enough about our faith to allow us to let it shine forth at home.

Parish personnel are waiting to be asked for help. They are familiar with the materials, the method, and the content to use with children. But they can't force us to ask them for help. We have to do that ourselves.

And if we're in a parish that hasn't as yet started family programs, we can begin doing some things on our own. In this book, I offer lessons, religious practices, paraliturgies, and other suggestions to help make religion part of family life. Let's not wait until "Father says so." Let's look at how fast our children are growing, tally up the amount of time we have left to pass on the Good News before they leave home, and make the decision today to become their primary religious educators.

CHAPTER 2

The Church and
the Family Calendar

I love turning the family calendar over to a new month. Its
clear whiteness attests to uncluttered days ahead, and the
vision of free time touches a need deep down somewhere.

But something happens directly after the page is
turned. Gremlins attack the white spaces and fill them
with phrases like "Mike—soccer—5:30" or "Jim—Board
Meeting—7:30" or "Dolor—Author's League." By the end of
the first week of the month the pristine whiteness is gone,
and by the third week we're all staring at it helplessly,
wondering how it filled up so fast.

In today's culture we live by the calendar and may
well perish by the calendar. At the end of every meeting,
attenders whip out their pocket calendars and try to find a
date to meet again in the far future. "I'll have to check my
calendar" is standard farewell fare today.

Whenever I'm asked which I prefer being called,
homemaker or housewife, I reply, "Neither. I'm a
coordinator." The family inherits everybody else's calendar.
After the officials and administrators and meeting-goers tuck
their little calendars back into their pockets, they take them
home and transfer the notations to the family's master
calendar—which also holds the endless schedules from
school, Little League, dentists, organizations, friends, and
church.

Often I hear pastors or religious educators, weary and
frustrated from unsuccessful efforts to get parents to come to
meetings, complain, "These parents just aren't interested.
They won't come to meetings. They say they want help and
courses, but when we offer them they won't show up."

I can understand their frustration, but I can also empathize with parents. Families are busy places today. It's highly likely that parents would very much like to be at a meeting but that on the same night as the meeting they have also been called to school for a conference or to a "very important" game in which one of their children is playing.

We have only three children, yet one Saturday we found ourselves in the absurd situation of being expected to be in five places simultaneously. Each of our boys had a soccer game, which "good" parents are expected to attend. Our high schooler had Band Day, which "good" parents watch and photograph. I had a diocesan "Call to Action" meeting, which "good" parishioners attend. And one of our sons had signed up for a booth at a crafts fair weeks ahead of the soccer schedule.

One "good" parent deposited and retrieved children while the other booth-sat. After that, we began turning down invitations for the following month and limiting our commitments to leagues and lessons. Gradually, however, they sneaked back onto the calendar. They always do.

In her Atlantic Richfield commercials, Lee Remick mentions that seventy-five percent of the American people want to return to a slower-paced, more pastoral life. She hopes that by our tricentennial that goal will be realized. So do I.

Meanwhile, however, we have to look for new ways to schedule God onto our family calendars. We don't always have to meet Monday nights from 7:30 to 10. We could try a Sunday brunch between Masses.

I once gave this recipe for religious education programs today:

Take thirty children.
Mix with one teacher.
Put in one classroom.
Bake for one hour each week.
Remove when done each spring.
If results are uneven, simply
rebake following fall—same
ingredients, same method.

Why must we repeat an old formula that today's families are finding harder and harder to follow? It's interesting to realize that Jesus never taught in a classroom on Monday nights from 7:30 to 8:30. He taught sometimes on mountaintops, sometimes from boats, sometimes walking from one city to another—in short, he utilized everyday teaching time.

It's time for us to consider some creative scheduling so that we utilize family time instead of infringing on it. Instead of sending youngsters to CCD once a week in the evening, let's consider setting up a total weekend of classes or a summer religion camp for them—and maybe for their families. Some dioceses have experienced great success in getting families to attend family vacation/retreats over the Fourth of July. During this long weekend, more religious instruction and experience is given the family than all year long, they tell me, and it's also the only time many families experience religion together in today's fragmented society.

The worst possible time for adult classes, which demand fresh thinking, is after dinner in the evening. By then, most adults have worked all day and have probably rushed dinner to get to class. There they sink into a glazed stupor, regardless of their desire to learn and understand. Morning classes for people who are free then and luncheon lectures for working adults are becoming more common and successful in parish adult education programs.

On a Monday morning of a three-day weekend, I was scheduled to speak in a Seattle airport hotel on the subject "Today's Woman and Her Church." The people attending were going to pay $1.75 for a roll, orange juice, coffee, and me. "I wonder if anyone will come," I feared aloud to the director of adult education who had invited me. She smiled.

They anticipated 150 and cut off the group at 200. Why did these people come out to the airport on a Monday morning when they could have been home with their families? For the same reason executives have business breakfasts. They were fresh, interested in the subject, and free to attend. They could get sitters, and they looked forward to it as a learning and socializing experience.

How wise that director of adult education! She saw the business breakfast as a viable learning opportunity for women as well as men.

In my own parish community, a Newman Center, we do some creative scheduling for our youth program. Recognizing the difficulty, if not impossibility, of getting teenagers out once a week during the school year, we set up four- or six-week courses three times a year and invite them to come to as many as they can. Most can make it to two sessions out of the three. If they're playing football, they can skip the fall series and take it in January, while their friends who took the course in September are working part-time renting ski equipment.

We also take advantage of the Days of Religious Experience offered by our Denver Archdiocesan Ministry to Public School Youth program. This office consistently offers these Days during school days and invites parents to release their youth from junior and senior high once or twice a year to take part in a whole day of learning, discussion, and liturgy. These days are popular and a good alternative to Monday-night learning.

We also utilize two other learning options. We hold one evening meeting a month for teenagers and their parents in one another's homes and schedule a Mass, potluck supper, and discussion. And we try to schedule a yearly "weekend" or retreat for our teenagers, away from the parish and with priests and counselors familiar with teaching teens today.

But teenagers aren't the only students. Families are the best students, and parishes are finding that Sunday mornings once or twice a month are a very good time to teach total family religion. (The Paulist *Family* program is based on such an approach.) Sundays are about the only time left for the family today, and Sunday afternoon football is rapidly encroaching upon half that day. Still, Sunday mornings can be family/church time, and parishes can be encouraged to utilize that time better for the family.

Protestants have long used Sunday mornings for educational purposes. I tend to think we've ignored that time because of our heavy Mass schedules and because in the past we left the setting up of programs to Father. Traditionally, Father was responsible for both Mass and religious education and couldn't do both at once. That has changed. Few pastors teach religious education, and most families prefer to devote the whole of Sunday morning to religious enrichment rather than come back three or four times during the week.

Parish mini-missions, summer overnights, and weekends are all attractive alternatives to fragmenting the family during the schoolyear week. Let's suggest some alternatives. As parents, let's offer to serve on the parish calendar board. Let's try some pilot programs to see if we can't have both: parents who are interested and parents who are there.

CHAPTER 3

"I Don't Know What I Believe"

At a faculty meeting, a teacher was asked her opinion on the subject at hand. She rambled on for awhile and then the chairman politely urged her to get to the nub of the subject. She turned to him and said, "I don't know what I think until I say it!"

This is a situation familiar to many Christian parents today. We aren't sure what we want of and for our children as far as religion is concerned, but we haven't had to face our uncertainty because we haven't had to express it.

When I work with parents in workshops, I find that few couples have discussed together what they themselves believe or what they want passed on to their children. Yet all good teaching must emanate from a philosophy. If not, that lack of philosophy becomes the lesson itself.

I like to ask workshop participants to begin by writing down their religious philosophy as parents by answering the question: "What do I want for my child out of religion?"

Some parents want primary emphasis put on doctrine, some on social activism. Still others want a cultural tradition that will be useful to their children in "getting ahead" but that won't hamper them in attaining that objective. At this early point in a workshop, the most important thing is not the content of the parents' answers but the self-knowledge they gain from scrutinizing and articulating their wants.

One couple came up with this religious philosophy:
1. We want our children to "feel" that as Catholics they are a chosen people. This means we want lots of family celebrations—wedding anniversaries, Advent, Saints' Days. We think that through celebrations our children will feel a sense of Christian community with each other and with the parish. We also hope it will enable them to celebrate Mass more fully.
2. We want them to learn to pray. This means we must help them become comfortable with prayer and let them see that we are comfortable with prayer and meditation.
3. We want them to have an understanding of their past: the symbols, songs, glory of their people, the suffering, the heroes, the villains, our glories, our failures. This means we must bring history to their level, and it means that we, as Catholic parents, must know more about Church history than we now do.
4. We want them to have a Christian concern for the welfare of others even if it means discomfort for us. This means we must accept all kinds of people—including their friends—, as different as they may be from our ideals.
5. We want them to behave morally according to the Judeo-Christian ethic, and we want them to internalize this, to behave morally not because of our rules or threats but because they believe it's God's way. We want them to obey God and live good lives because they love him, not because they fear him.
6. We want them to know the value of faith, to know that all people throughout time have needed to believe in something and in a Creator of some sort. This means they must be aware of other religions and gods and wonder why we think ours is the true one. Also, it means they must see the difference faith makes in our lives.
7. We want them eventually to make a commitment to God and, hopefully, to Catholicism on their own part (not ours).
8. We want to review this philosophy together each year to see if we're accomplishing our goals.

Actually, the couple mentioned above didn't have to wait a year. A second part of our workshop deals with

16

methods of achieving the goals stated in the couples' Catholic parenting philosophy. This couple took their eight stated hopes and then made very practical plans for how to achieve them. Finally, they took their family calendars and scheduled their practical plans onto them. In this way today's families can achieve real results.

A second problem concerns those parents whose religious beliefs have changed since marriage. Back in the chaos of the sixties, someone defined a high school teacher as that person designated by the rest of us to make sense out of our society and to justify our role in it.

If we paraphrase it, we have a pretty fair definition of the religion teacher: that person designated by us to make sense out of our Church and religion and to reconcile our religious behavior with that explanation.

Many parents today want the Church to continue teaching what they themselves have come to ignore. Many of us won't even examine our beliefs because we fear, or we know, they've changed and we don't want to face the possibility that we might not be truly Catholic.

It's easier to wonder why someone else isn't passing on the faith than to scrutinize the dichotomy between what we were taught and what our actions announce that we believe.

Just for starters, here's a self-scrutiny quiz. I used it in my column "Talks to Parents," which goes into two million homes, and was startled at the number of letters I received about it. Many parents took the test individually and then shared it with their spouse, a format I had suggested. However, they went on to share it with their pastor, their directors of religious education, and even me.

Apparently the quiz struck a nerve and started many couples and groups of couples thinking and talking. The interesting part about my readers' reactions was that they were relieved to face some of their disbeliefs. It was almost as if they were thanking me for bringing them out into the open.

A Little Test on Beliefs
by Dolores Curran

1. I believe in (heaven) (hell) (purgatory) (limbo). I want my children taught to believe (the same) (something different). What difference do I want?
Note: Repeat sentences two and three of the above question after each of the test questions.
2. I believe that those who are divorced and remarried (are) (are not) living in a state of sin.
3. I believe that it (is) (is not) sinful to disagree with (the Pope) (my bishop) (my pastor) on matters of faith and morals.
4. I believe that everyday racism (is) (is not) sinful.
5. I believe that it (is) (is not) sinful to indulge in servile work on Sundays.
6. I believe that the Sacrament of Reconciliation (is) (is not) an important sacrament and should be received

_____.
      (how often)
7. I believe that it (is) (is not) sinful to wilfully miss Sunday Mass.
8. I believe that artificial contraception (is) (is not) sinful.
9. I believe that it (is) (is not) my duty to pass on religious beliefs to my children whether I believe them or not.
10. I (believe) (do not believe) that I need to think more about my beliefs.

This little quiz wasn't designed to steal sleep from already-harassed Catholic parents but to force them to face up to a foolish mentality that says we can expect our Church to continue teaching our children things that we ourselves may have come to question.

Children can't respond to moral teaching when they receive a double set of messages, one from their Church and one from their parents. This confusion surfaces both in religion class and in daily life, where values are brought into play.

Parents who think they don't have the problem need to ask themselves if their budding adolescents have ever questioned them about their attitudes on abortion, mercy killing, racism, contraception, heaven/hell/purgatory, divorce, and remarriage. It's likely that, being perceptive as only offspring can be, some children sense that these are areas too uncomfortable for their parents to discuss.

Often, too, parents disagree on morality, and because they want to hide that disagreement from their children, the subject becomes taboo in the home. I don't think it's exaggerating much to say that most of the major issues of today are discussed not in the Catholic family but in religion class and Catholic newspapers.

What a pity! Of what value are moral teachings and thinking if they can't even be discussed between parents and youth? We avoid such frank discussions because our teenagers might well disagree with us and with our Church. This avoidance may keep peace between us, but it doesn't help either parents or children to formulate and evaluate moral choices.

I commend those parents who are courageous enough to bring up subjects like premarital sex, peace, and divorce, knowing that their children will disagree with them. Even if such parents aren't changing attitudes, at least they're talking about the issues. And they and their young adults are listening to one another, a process which sets the foundation for further valuing and discussing as time goes on.

This brings me back to the beginning of this chapter. Good teaching doesn't spring from emptiness. If we haven't decided what we want to pass along to our children, that indecision is what we're passing along. And that's the deposit of faith many Catholic children are getting today.

CHAPTER 4

Where Are the Catholic Fathers?

"There will be a parents' meeting on Thursday evening at 7 o'clock. The mothers of our primary children will meet in the hall, and the mothers of our teenagers will meet in the cafeteria." Midwest bulletin

"An analysis of the parochial school data by my colleague, William McCready, leaves no doubt at all that the most important predictor of religious performance of children is the religious behavior of their parents (and particularly their fathers) and the quality of the relationship between their mothers and fathers." Andrew Greeley, *The New Agenda*

"Well, maybe if we feed the men, give them a steak dinner or something, they'll come back." Parish council meeting, Los Angeles

"Don't be surprised if few fathers show up for meetings. To counteract this, set up the meetings with intellectual and psychological interest and provide an atmosphere of open discussion." Religion textbook, 1971

"Religion is really a woman's sphere. If my wife didn't take religion seriously, I suppose I'd enroll the kids in the parish school." Jesuit-educated dentist, Spokane

This chapter concerns the missing link in religious education: the Catholic dad. For a long time, catechists have suspected the importance of the father to the religious formation of the child. Now there is data proving that he might be the single most important element in our children's religious life, followed closely by the quality of the relationship between him and his spouse. A 1963 study by Andrew Greeley and William McCready at the National Opinion Research Center (NORC), reanalyzed and fortified with new data, indicates that parental religious behavior, particularly that of the father, is the prime factor in determining the child's eventual religious behavior.

In *The New Agenda* (Doubleday Image), Father Greeley writes:

> I do not know how William McCready's findings will be received when they are published. My hunch is that they will be ignored, because they are both a judgment on the optimism of professional educators and an awesome threat to parents.
>
> The elaborate statistical models he has developed leave no doubt at all that the parent is not only the principal educator but so important as an educator that all other educational institutions might almost be considered marginal in comparison.

If such data holds up, then most of our religious education efforts with children are secondary. The miles of print and hours of lectures concerning religion texts, teacher training, parochial school, CCD, and various episcopal documents are marginal. In words which will endear him to a parent's heart, Father Greeley described the researcher's own feelings:

> Professor McCready, who has an infant son, tells me that he was badly shaken by his own findings. For, as he put it, his models told him that what was going on at home at night in the primal triad of him, his wife, and their bright-eyed offspring was the most important educational experience that that young man will ever have in all his life.

These same NORC findings led Bishop Cletus F. O'Donnell of Madison to tell chief administrators of Catholic education,

"If you want to educate the next generation, you must at the same time educate the present generation." The bishop added that because both sons and daughters "are more heavily influenced religiously by their fathers than by their mothers, religious education programs dealing with the family unit must be especially concerned with the father."

Yet we find ourselves without active Catholic fathers. We see the strong Tevyes in conservative Jewish congregations. We recognize the strength of the Mormon family, where the father is truly the spiritual leader. We note that in almost all growing sects, such as Jehovah Witnesses, the male is a primary religious factor, both in the home and in the church.

But when we Catholics call a parish meeting, we count eighty percent women. Worse, we expect it. We spend hours devising ways to lure Catholic males into involvement in the simplest religious activity. The deviousness of such attempts turns many women off. As one woman put it, "If we have to resort to feeding or entertaining the men just to get them to be part of their family's religious life, then they become our children, too."

How did we reach this point in our Church? We know that, following the Jewish tradition referred to earlier, the married male played a strong role in the early Christian community. Through him, religion was passed on via legend, instruction, and example. Because his home was male-dominated, he accepted the spiritual responsibility as naturally as he accepted economic responsibility.

This responsibility gradually eroded in Europe to the point where religion became a woman's thing. Anyone who has ever attended Mass in one of the Latin countries gets the impression that, except for activity around the altar, Catholicism is distinctly matriarchial. Only on high feast days—Mardi Gras in France, Semana Santa in Spain, St. Joseph's Day in Italy—do the men take active roles, and then it's the visible roles only.

Immigration hastened this erosion of the male's religious leadership and example in the family. Occupied with learning new language, customs, and technology, our forefathers spent their energies making a living for their families. Religion was left to mother and eventually institutionalized in the school. After decades of solidifying these two "institutions," our Catholic men came to see their role as twofold: marry the good Catholic woman and supply parochial school tuitions.

Our acceptance of these roles surfaced a bit of folklore regarding the mixed marriage: it was better for a Catholic girl to marry a non-Catholic boy than the reverse because, if the mother was Catholic, at least the kids were saved.

Finally, to compound the erosion, there was until recently a growing cultural attitude in our country that religion was unmasculine. When and why this started is uncertain, but our history tells us that our early political leaders, military men, and settlers considered religion a manly trait. Old letters and documents attest to the openness with which men spoke of God, prayer, and faith. Gradually, this openness diminished to the point where men who exhibited religious devotion were considered less masculine than those who turned it over to women. "Manly" men worked hard to control all emotions and cover up any sign of religious emotion. Just a glance at the ordinary parish handshake of peace shows how well they passed down this control.

Fortunately, this trend is reversing itself. The kids of the sixties rediscovered feelings and religion, and today we find a return to religion as a manly art. Businessmen are meeting for prayer. Sports figures are joining Christian athletic groups. Military cadets are meditating. But we have far to go before we can wipe out the legacy passed on from father to son: "Religion is a woman's thing."

How do we attack the problem of the Catholic male missing from our faith processes? We need a two-pronged approach: reinvolve the men, and help the women handle the missing-male problem.

The first step in reinvolving lay males calls for creating an awareness of the problem in our Church. We need to face the missing-male situation squarely and constantly. Pastors tend to talk about it timidly and apologetically for fear of offending male feelings. The general thrust in the past has been to emphasize to women the importance of their responsibility in getting men to church. Then, if they failed, they accepted the guilt and the gentle chidings of pastor and principal.

Few new women accept this kind of responsibility. "It's not my job to nag my husband to a parents' meeting," said one mother during her local parish meeting. "The kids and the faith belong to both of us, and I refuse to be a Catholic Portnoy's mother." The women who were present applauded.

In the light of the NORC findings, which are covered more fully in Greeley's book, *The Catholic School in a Declining Church* (Sheed and Ward), the reinvolvement of the Catholic lay male is an obvious topic for the agendas of the bishops' meetings, pastoral councils, seminary curricula, Catholic periodicals, religious education meetings, columns, homilies, and bulletins. Quite simply, we have to give to it the same importance we gave to Catholic education.

And the father has to be educated to his importance in the religious education process. Two years ago, when I spoke on the subject at the Los Angeles Congress of Religious Education, one man listened to the discussion swirling about him and then made this admission, "I've got to admit I never before realized I was basically important to my children's religion. Sure, I heard the pulpit pleas and all that, but I never knew there was solid data pointing to me as the most important religious personage in my children's lives. That's pretty frightening."

Our men do *not* know their importance in the religious development process. But their role is so basic that a parish might do well to call a moratorium on traditional CCD classes for a year in order to concentrate personnel, resources, and expertise on reactivating the major factor in the child's education: the Catholic dad. He can't be blamed for underestimating his importance if he isn't aware of it; and that awareness—a consciousness-raising—requires total Church effort.

In this effort, we need to rid ourselves of telltale phrases such as "the Catholic parent, she... ," which are unconscious exposures of the kind of conditioning we've accepted, that the mother is the most important religious educator. Constant reminders from bulletin and pulpit, prayers during Mass, and reports on male attendance can all become a part of parish education if the leadership is tuned into the importance of the effort.

A second step is to furnish some Male-Only meetings.
When couples attend parent meetings, the men tend to sit mutely and defer to the women. After dealing with this frustrating dilemma a number of years, I came to realize it stems from many causes: embarrassment, ignorance, resentment, and even a refusal to face up to growing unbelief.

In an attempt to deal with these feelings, I have divided men and women into separate groups during workshops to give the men an opportunity to examine their own attitudes and ventilate their own feelings at being asked to become a real part of spiritual parenthood. With the exception of the first, a trial run, I have not taken part in Men-Only workshops, but I have listened to tapes of them. It is far better to have an involved layman lead the session than either a woman or a priest.

Following is an Attitude Quiz I developed to force men to examine their own religious attitudes. There are no right or wrong answers, and the quiz is not a scientific survey but a trigger to get men talking. I encourage them to pass over any questions they dislike and to answer the others as quickly as possible.

Some of the answers that turn up again and again show the depth of our problem in activating the Catholic male. There's enough material to launch a dozen sermons. Question #1, for instance, exhibits that many men feel women are more religious than men "because they like that sort of thing," and, "mothers are better at it than fathers." In some groups, the shocker is question #6, which forces men to scrutinize their own religiosity. Many admit that if their wives weren't interested in religion, they wouldn't be either, a situation that led one participant to say, "I guess I'm finally facing my lack of belief."

Questions #7 and #8 indicate quite clearly that men tend to mimic their father's religious behavior even if they disapproved of it.

Religious Attitude Quiz
by Dolores Curran

(May be reproduced for parish use only.)
1. Women are more religious than men because _____
_____ .
2. I would feel _____ leading my family in a religious celebration.
3. I think men become priests because _____
_____ .
4. I (would) (would not) want to be a deacon because _____
_____ .
5. The children's religious upbringing should be the mother's job because _____ .
6. If my wife didn't take religion seriously, I would _____
_____ .
7. My one-sentence description of my father's religious behavior: _____
_____ .
8. My religious behavior (is about the same as) (is less enthusiastic than) (is more mature than) my father's.
9. In a mixed marriage, it is better that the (husband) (wife) be Catholic because _____ .
10. In 20 years, my son will sum up my religiosity like this:
_____ .

A third step calls for a dimension to the religious life of a couple that isn't directly related to marriage and family. So many of our efforts center on family that they tend to foster the mentality that religion isn't of much interest to a man unless he has a family. Yet couples who do take a course in comparative religion, or attend a lecture series or weekend retreat on changing theology, find religion has an exciting added dimension, one which can generate lively discussion between husband and wife.

Some parishes send couples to their annual diocesan religious education congresses along with their religion teachers, paying travel, hotel, and registration costs, just to give the couples a wider scope of religion. This is wise use of educational monies on the part of parish council or leadership. When couples get turned on to theology, prayer, and the myriad of other religious subjects offered at various workshops and conventions, they tend to get turned on to parish involvement, and the men see religion as something more exciting than just First Communion preparation.

We need, too, to reevaluate traditional parish social groupings which segregate men from women, old from young, singles from couples, and clergy from laity. The Altar Society and Knights of Columbus of old deliberately separated us from one another so effectively that we came to stereotype the members by the group's activity. Couples came to believe they were fulfilling a religious responsibility by playing bridge or listening to a coach. Most of the parish organizations for men degenerated into a smoker mentality. The main purpose became the entertainment, and the program chairman became the chief functionary. Occasionally the group was called upon to run bingo or to set up bazaar booths, but rarely to think about religion or to pray.

What happens when women begin studying religion seriously? When eight out of ten participants at a religious lecture series are women, there are a lot of families in which the wives are outdistancing their husbands in religious thinking. O. W. Holmes said, "Once a mind is stretched by a new idea, it can never return to its original dimension." When I see women's minds stretching, I wonder about the effect upon their spiritual relationship with their husbands.

28

If a man lives by his early parochial school concept of Church and his wife by a broader concept of Church introduced by speakers or writers like McBrien, Brown, and Baum, there has to be frustration, if not friction. This frustration surfaced in one of my talks in Seattle. The first comment came from a woman. "Every time I come to a workshop like this, I get excited about my faith and my life, but then I go home to a husband and teenagers who think I'm weird for wanting to come in the first place."

How do we help women handle this all-too-common situation in today's Catholic home? This calls for the second prong of our effort: helping women handle the uncooperative spiritual spouse. Ignoring the problem leads to the risky situation in which the woman's religious growth puts a strain on the marriage itself.

First, women must be encouraged to share their honest feelings with husbands. A good number of men don't know that their wives wish they could share a religious relationship. Their wives may be seething inside, but they aren't communicating it.

"I didn't know it was that important to you" is a common husbandly response reported by wives who do take the step of exposing their feelings on this subject.

Catholic women in the past were conditioned to prod a man into a religious activity but cautioned not to push too hard. "Ask him to do it for you" was retreat advice. In retrospect, some of our wifely religious behavior was downright insulting to both the Catholic man and the Catholic woman. He was handled not like an adult but like a child who has to be cajoled into going to Sunday School.

That overt behavior is gone, but its residue keeps many women from sharing their real feelings with their husbands. If a woman admires, even envies, a spiritually united couple, she can admit frankly to her husband, "I wish we had that kind of relationship. I really envy them." This admission is bound to open up the discussion and expose some feelings that might be surprisingly positive on the part of the husband.

Women also need to let their resentments surface. If a woman resents her husband's bland presumption that she is the one to attend the parish meeting, she can say, "I'm beginning to feel some strong anger on this. Our kids have two parents who profess to be Christian. Why is their religion my job? I get angry every time I go to one of these meetings alone and see other couples there. Why must I go alone?"

A husband may be astonished and defensive, but eventually he must reflect upon his wife's words, a reflection that won't happen as long as she keeps her feelings hidden. I have seen many relationships take on a new depth when the wife became honest with her spouse regarding religion in the home. It's a long, and in some cases, a futile process, but it can't begin without openness.

Secondly, women need to help men become comfortable with prayer and celebration. To women who have been culturally allowed to exhibit emotion, men's reticence is hard to understand. Some wives refuse to accept it and will set up an elaborate Paschal meal or neighborhood Mass, expecting their husbands to lead the spiritual show. When their husbands fail to respond, the women shrug, "Well, I tried that, but my husband wasn't interested."

Some men find it difficult even to lead a decade of the rosary. I don't think they should be patronized, but neither should they be forced to react spontaneously and energetically to open prayer, song, and celebration.

When I give celebration workshops, I suggest shared prayer and celebrations rather than a father-led paraliturgy. Children are very good at celebrating, and their naturalness often makes an otherwise-uptight dad comfortable. If each member takes a portion of a Lenten liturgy, say a family Stations of the Cross, Dad becomes a participant, not a mini-priest.

Parishes can help by offering demonstration home liturgies and practice prayer sessions. I witnessed a parish that used my filmstrip and sample handout family-celebration sheets (*Family Celebrations for Religious*

Education, 23rd Publications) to instill a group feeling of celebration prior to trying it out at home. Under the skillful hand of the Director of Religious Education, the pilot liturgies practiced by Mom and Dad in class enthused many to try them at home.

Likewise, little groups of families getting together to hold an Advent ceremony or home Mass help take the discomfort off the single male leader in the family. One of the real pluses in any parish celebration effort is getting such families in contact with one another.

Finally, we need to help women accept their aloneness in the religious life of their homes. Some men may never become active spiritually, and the wife is left with the option of either constantly trying to involve him or going on without him. She sees other families in which the unit is religiously whole, and she wants desperately to give that to her family.

What's she to do? Go on alone, always keeping the option open for her husband but not using her major energies and emotions on that effort. She and the rest of the family are more important. If Dad refuses to be part of a family or school religious function, she and the children must go ahead. If the children question Dad's absence, she can have them transfer the question to him. It's usually more difficult for a father to answer to his children than to his wife for his religious indifference.

Predictably, the sons will want to follow his example and withdraw themselves, so a mother should offset this eventuality by showing the boys other male models who participate in religious activity. It is then imperative to get together with other celebrating families or to get involved in some type of parish family program.

The great temptation is to give up. Many women use their spouses' inaction as a reason for their own, thereby effectively cutting off the opportunity for change on the part of the children. It is better if the mother continues with a strong religious environment in the home without making an issue out of the father's lack of interest. Eventually some men become involved, particularly if they are ignored. Others don't, but the family's spiritual life goes on without them.

I can't finish this chapter without mentioning the special problems of single parents and mix-marrieds. The NORC information can have a depressing effect upon mothers who are already trying to rear Catholic children alone. If the father is the major predictor and the quality of the marriage the second, it renders the separated and widowed mother almost weaponless from the start. Again the best answer lies in combining families in some sort of clustering group.

Some parishes deliberately structure groups or clusters to include a variety of family makeups— two-parent families, father-only and mother-only families, widows, widowers, and other singles. These benefit all involved. Children from mother-only families can interact with men, and those from father-only families with women other than teachers, sitters, and grandmothers. All the children have an opportunity, often lacking in nuclear families, to relate to a variety of adults, and the adults themselves share supportive relationships.

Also, more parishes are tuning into the special needs of the divorced Catholic parent by forming local groups similar to Parents Without Partners. They hold small home Masses for families and offer some counseling help for parents alone, not to mention the psychological support such groups offer. On a national scale, there is the North American Conference for Separated and Divorced Catholics, which brings such Catholics together for mutual support and spirituality. Information can be obtained through diocesan Family Life Bureaus.

The mixed-married have different problems and needs. I was once misquoted in the Catholic press as saying that the mixed-married had better spiritual marriages than the totally Catholic couple. What I really said was that mixed-married partners often have a better idea of what they believe and what they want spiritually for themselves and their families because they are forced to discuss it. This doesn't mean they agree. Often the Catholic parent feels lonely, a loneliness which may easily grow into resentment.

Some mixed-married couples are able to function well as religious cooperators in the home. Theology doesn't interfere with family prayer and celebration as much as it does with church prayer and celebration. I'm frequently surprised, though, to meet a Catholic spouse who presumes the non-Catholic spouse doesn't want anything to do with family religious activity. "Did you invite him (her)?" I'll ask.

"No, I don't want to push him (her), you know."

Maybe he or she's waiting for an invitation. Mixed-marrieds who have become partners and share in bringing the faith home tell me there is sometimes too much consideration for the other's faith, to the point that invitations aren't offered and the non-Catholic spouse feels left out.

I notice that mixed-marrieds tend to gather together at parents' workshops, and I wonder if the time isn't ripe for some workshops and retreats that specialize solely in the needs and spirituality of the Catholic mixed-marrieds. Generally speaking, if the father is active in any denomination, his children tend to respond to their own religion more than if he embraces none. In one sense, then, a strong religious belief on the part of a Protestant father can serve the Catholic child. There are, of course, offsetting tensions that can render this kind of service void.

Each mixed-married couple is unique. A mixed marriage can include a religion-filled home; a Catholic marriage can become a spiritually broken home where the father is there but indifferent.

The future? I see hopeful signs of reinvolving the lay male in our Church. He is being prodded by his spiritual emptiness, his family, and his Church to become a real spiritual leader in the family, not the mythical one we've pretended existed all these years. His Church is recognizing his unique role at last, and his world is calling for Christian witness. How he responds to this call is to be seen, but the summons is out.

CHAPTER 5

Birds, Bees, Parents, Kids, and You-Know-What

One of those newspaper items destined to give parents a wry smile recently announced statistics from the Department of Health, Education, and Welfare (HEW) that childhood now officially ends at twelve. I suppose such information is needed for programs and budgets, but few parents are so rash as to conclude that childhood ever ends. So much evidence contradicts it!

But the sobering side of the HEW report is that the mean age during which most children enter puberty has moved from sixteen to twelve in just three generations. This means that the pace and needs of our twelve-year-old children approximate those of their great-grandparents when they were sixteen. This is no secret to parents, of course. We know our children are growing up fast—too fast to give them all the skills, values, and information we feel they need to cope with life today.

If most of our children stop being children by twelve, two factors have to be considered in any kind of parental teaching: 1) parents must pack in more information faster because childhood is shortened, and 2) parents and teenagers must cope with emerging sexuality longer because adolescence is lengthened. It's a case of the bigger the field, the shorter the hoe.

This leads directly to the question, "How and when do we teach children about sex and sexuality?" From the miles of newsprint espousing and condemning sex education in our schools, one damning statistic stands out: only twelve percent of all parents (or one out of eight) teach any kind of sex information at all. According to a study called The Gilbert Youth Survey, which studied the source of sex education, seventy-five percent of our young people learn about sex from friends, twelve percent from parents, eight percent from reading and media, four percent from school, and one percent from other sources. Consistently we hear parents say, "Sex education is our right and responsibility, not the school's or the Church's." Yet only twelve percent actually do any teaching.

A survey asking the question, "Who should teach children about sex?" found parents evenly divided, one-third answering school, one-third Church, and one-third parents. However, only a third of those who felt that parents should teach children about sex admitted feeling capable of carrying out the role of sex educator. Why?

Why do we insist that nobody else interfere with our right to pass on such sensitive and personal information as that about sex and then do nothing about it ourselves? Why do we fool ourselves with that deluding "Our children never asked about sex, so I guess they weren't interested" stance? Why will we put more energy into fighting someone else's sex ed program than into furnishing something—anything —ourselves?

There are reasons why. Today's parent is the limbo parent, caught between two generations. One had all the answers, and the other accepts none. We find ourselves simultaneously labeled modernistic by our parents' generation and obsolete by our children's. Caught in the controversy between the two, we tend to do nothing. And that's what our children are getting from us: nothing. Yet never before have we so needed to give them information and moral education to offset the cultural images they're receiving today.

Perhaps a good place to start is with our own attitudes.

Here is a simple attitude quiz I use with parents during workshops. There are no right or wrong answers.

The questions serve only to help us face our own attitudes. If you are comfortable enough to discuss these in a group with other parents, it's an excellent way to learn from one another and to give some help and insights to wavering parents.

Sex Education Attitude Quiz
by Dolores Curran

1. I am teaching my children about sex in the same way my parents taught me. (true) (false)
2. It would embarrass me to discuss sex with my child in front of my spouse. (true) (false)
3. I distrust sex education in schools because it is a political move designed to control my child's mind. (true) (false)
4. If parents answer their children's questions on sex when the questions arise, that is sufficient sex education. (true) (false)
5. If children know all about sex, they won't get into trouble. (true) (false)
6. I can teach my children about contraception without going into the morality of it. (true) (false)
7. Television is more harmful than helpful in teaching our children about sex. (true) (false)
8. I think that sex should be taught only in the context of marriage. (true) (false)
9. If it embarrasses me to talk about sex with my children, it is better to have someone else do it. (true) (false)
10. Schools are better sex educators than parents. (true) (false)

In discussing your answers, here are some points to ponder.

1. I am teaching my children about sex in the same way my parents taught me. Parents tend to rear children as they themselves were reared even if they disapprove of that method. If today's parents were taught about sex with an embarrassed curtness, they're apt to teach it in the same way, unless they make a conscious effort to change. If they were taught about it by parents who regarded sex reverently as a gift from God, they're apt to teach it that way. If they were taught about it only as an adjunct to the Sixth Commandment, they might well pass on that attitude. Probably the final consideration is "Did I like the way my parents approached sexuality and sex, and did it meet my needs?" The answer to that question should determine whether the parents mimic or change the methods used by their parents.

2. It would embarrass me to discuss sex with my child in front of my spouse. Many couples discuss everything together but sex. Dad peels son off to the den, and Mom takes daughter into the bedroom to talk about it. If sex is a beautiful, holy thing between husband and wife, why do they need to be apart while discussing it with their children? Discuss whether or not it might be better for brothers and sisters to hear about sex together from both parents—perhaps in a home religion lesson—rather than separated, simply because that's the way it's always been done in the schools.

3. I distrust sex education in schools because it is a political move designed to control my child's mind. Discuss the origins of this fear and whether or not it is justified on your mature level of thinking today. Did it come out of the fifties when everything, including the fluoridation of water, was considered to be Communist-inspired? Have the programs available to you been endorsed by highly respected leaders, bishops, and superintendents, and if so, what information do you have that they would allow subversive programs to flourish under the title of sex education? Rampant fear is catching, but like most communicable disease, it belongs in childhood.

4. If parents answer their children's questions on sex when they arise, that is sufficient sex education. *How* do they answer them? If it's evasively or with partial truths, the children won't ask the next question. If it's with embarrassment, the children will sense that, too, and will avoid putting parents through it again. If it's with honesty and sometimes an admission of ignorance, the children will be encouraged to discuss their questions and misunderstandings with their parents.

And what happens if the children don't ask? One popular excuse parents give for inaction is that their children never showed any interest. I think it's a fair generalization that all children are interested in sex. Therefore, if they don't ask, parents need to bring up the subject during the numerous opportunities offered in today's culture.

5. If children know all about sex, they won't get into trouble. One family psychologist calls this one of the myths of parenthood. Many parents want sex education for negative reasons—to prevent pregnancy, to avoid VD, to show the harmful effects of drugs, to minimize the attraction of an early marriage. Teaching about sex alone without teaching about responsibility, love, morality, and commitment to others is foolish and even counterproductive. Some parents want biology teachers to teach the biology of sex but want to reserve the morality of it for themselves. Others want to be responsible for it all, but again, only twelve percent actually fulfill this responsibility. Where do you stand?

6. I can teach my children about contraception without going into the morality of it. Thousands of Catholic parents are trying to do this today, and they are sending their children double messages: contraception is wrong, but don't worry about it. Honesty is basic in teaching children about sex. If parents aren't going to sweep the contraception issue under the bed, and thereby close communication with their children on it, they are going to have to discuss the whole subject with them: methods and morality of contraception from the Church's, culture's, world's, and—most importantly—parents' point of view. If parents' attitude differs from the Church's, then the parents must note and discuss the differences. They can't expect the Church to successfully teach their children what they themselves no longer believe.

7. Television is more harmful than helpful in teaching our children about sex. Parents realize the powerful role television plays in forming children's attitudes toward materialism, crime, violence, sex, and marriage, but they aren't sure just how to control this influence. Is it better to turn it off, or to use it as a point of origin for discussion? Television provides us with excellent horrible examples (and a few good ones) of behavior, conduct, and personal values. By commenting on these and using them as a basis of discussion, we can inculcate some Christian values of our own. Studies show that it is better to watch together and make value judgments than to turn the TV off. The worst action, of course, is to allow children to watch unlimited television without the parents' being aware of what they are viewing.

8. I think that sex should be taught only in the context of marriage. Today's ten-year-olds are asking questions that must be answered even if they won't be interested in marriage for many years. (At ten, most likely, they vow never to marry.) The old practice of waiting until the senior year in high school to teach youngsters about sex because it fits into the marriage preparation course is foolish today. Television, movies, and peer influence make our children aware of sex at an early age, and they want their questions answered. We need both: ongoing sexuality education to meet the needs of the child at different ages, and intensive marriage preparation when that need arises.

9. If it strongly embarrasses me to talk about sex with my children, it is better to have someone else do it. If embarrassment hampers parents' discussion of sex with their children, then they must look to their own needs before their children's. They must discover why they are so embarrassed and work with a counselor, pastor, or clinician on ways to overcome this embarrassment so that they can become effective sex educators in their families. Such embarrassment is a clear signal that the parents need remedial sex education, and I hope parishes have some resources available for such parents.

10. Schools are better sex educators than parents are. Some schools are probably better than some parents and vice versa. Regardless of who is the best, both need to be involved, complementing one another. The parent is best equipped to teach morality, values, and reverence for sex. The school is best equipped to teach about parts of the body and their functions and general physiology. It doesn't have to be an either/or situation; it can be a both/and situation, as it is in most good education.

Sex Education and the TV Set

We were watching TV one evening when the subject matter became "mature"—a media euphemism for raunchy—, and my husband and I glanced at one another with that familiar parent message, "Do you think our watching child understands this?"

Before we had a chance to change channels, said child remarked, "You know, I don't understand this program." We glanced at each other in relief until our child continued, "Is that woman a prostitute, or a pusher?"

Our relief was both naive and short-lived. Today's child is subjected to a barrage of dramas involving VD, pornography, abortion, rape, homosexuality, extramarital affairs, and other "mature" subjects that boggle the parents' minds. We all came face-to-face with such images and ideas, but later in life, not at age eight or ten.

How can we turn the TV set around and use it as an aid in implanting healthy and moral attitudes toward sex? Well, as a cynic once said, "Everyone is in the world for a purpose, even if it's only to serve as a horrible example." Television presents us with enough horrible examples to fill a year's curriculum in teaching about the problems and morality of sex. But many of us don't know how to use the set. In another chapter I discuss that more fully.

Meanwhile, let's take an embarrassing family moment that can be an opportunity in disguise. The family is viewing a situation comedy. Without warning, the teenage daughter in the comedy hops into bed with her boy friend, and the camera roams the room as ecstatic sounds come from the vicinity of the bed.

How can the parents react? Here are some options: 1) They can sit in silence, all members of the family staring hard at the set, hoping the commercial will come soon. 2) A parent can stand up and snap off the set without a word. 3) The parents can condemn the incident as sinful pre-marital sex and stop the children from watching it. 4) The parents can ask the children how they feel about the incident and use it as a springboard for clarifying values.

The latter is obviously the most effective teaching tool, but one that is awkward for many parents. So often we tend to moralize when we really want to discuss. It's tempting to judge the action and let the silence lie there in the family.

Far better if Mom asks, "Do you suppose she really wanted to do that, or was she afraid she'd lose her boy friend if she didn't?" If the silence still lies there, Dad can come in with an answer, "She didn't seem very fond of him an hour ago."

If the silence persists, Mom and Dad can continue the discussion without even looking at the children, who are sitting there wondering if their parents have an ulterior motive in the discussion. Once satisfied that it's simply their parents' discussion, the children will break into it. (We all know the best way to call the children is to whisper together.)

Parents might practice this kind of "invitation to discuss" before TV situations arise. What they are doing is opening morality, especially but not solely sexual morality, as a family discussion topic, and lots of good attitudes can be implanted in that way.

42

Where Can Parents Get Help?

"I don't want the schools to teach my children about sex, but I don't know how to do it myself," a reader wrote me. "Where can we get help?"

We parents are rarely trained to be parents, especially sex-educating parents. Yet we're expected to carry out this function with confidence and ease. We learned about the immorality of subjects before we knew what they were, whereas our children are more familiar with the subjects than with the morality involved.

Morality is the most neglected part of sex education. It's no exaggeration to say that most of our children will get no moral education on sex unless we parents give it to them. Public schools, while adept at teaching the physiology, are legally prevented from touching on morality in sex and marriage.

Few religion teachers feel comfortable teaching the Sixth Commandment today, and who will blame them? Catholic parents are as divided among themselves as are non-Catholic parents on the morality of such subjects as divorce, contraception, and personal chastity. Pretending that there is only one Catholic stance on these issues is taking an ostrich approach when our children need help.

There's no longer one simple Catholic answer but lots of "It depends." Ultimately, of course, it depends on the parents. Children grow, shaped more by the culture than by the Church, and it's left to the home to reconcile the two.

So we parents have to update our moral education, examining our own attitudes on sexual morality. Am I going to teach my children that the remarried Catholic down the street is living in a state of mortal sin? Or am I going to teach them that the Church says he or she is but that I don't think that he or she is? Or am I, along with thousands of fellow parents, going to sort of let that one slide by?

I suggest that parents sit down together or with other couples and discuss those areas in which they need more help and then approach their pastor with specific requests. We can't blame Father for not giving us help if we leave it to him to guess our needs. Here are some areas which some parent groups have asked for help with from their parishes.

What should we teach? Give us someone who can speak to what should be taught—physically, emotionally, and morally—at a given age. This might be a theologian-physician pair or the pastor and biology teacher teaming up for an evening.

How do we teach? Give us some sample lessons and some demonstration teaching so that we will feel more confident when we open the subject at home.

What materials are available to us? A very minimal service of the parish should be a bibliography of sex education materials available in the parish, diocesan, and local libraries. A book exhibit is helpful. Filmstrips on sex education for parents as well as for children are often available through public schools. Parents will read materials of value to them and their children if they are aware of them.

Sexual morality today. What has changed since we were children? Give us a theologian versed in such problems as X-rated movies. We who spent whole retreats discussing French kissing never dreamed we'd be discussing venereal disease, pornography, and "mature" literature with our young teenagers. Give us some homilies and classes updating our moral theology.

Give us some parent classes and some self-help groups. Put those of us who want to give our children some worthwhile moral and physical sex education in touch with one another. Don't get distracted by the vocal parents who don't want it —and don't want us to have it, either.

Following are some worthwhile recordings, filmstrips, and books on sexuality and the parent:

Recordings and Filmstrips

Right, Wrong, or What? by Peter L. Steinke; a 38-minute tape of youths discussing sexual standards, personal relationships, marriage, parents, and the Church; Concordia Publishing House, St. Louis, Missouri.

Sex Education for Parents by Dolores Curran; tape recording; discusses ways and means of educating parents within the parish structure; N.C.R. Cassettes, Kansas City, Missouri.

Sex Is a Parent Affair; book and/or cassette; G/L Regal Books, Glendale, California 91209.

Parents As Sex Educators by Dolores Curran; motivational parish filmstrip with support materials for parent groups; 23rd Publications, West Mystic, Connecticut.

Books

Are You There, God? It's Me, Margaret by Judy Blume; good for girls nearing puberty; reflects their fears and lives in fictional form with a twelve-year-old girl as main character; Dell Publishing, New York.

Better Than the Birds, Smarter Than the Bees by Helen J. Burn; Abingdon Press, New York.

A Boy's Sex Life by William J. Bausch; Fides Publishers, Notre Dame, Indiana.

Diary of a Young Girl by Anne Frank; exposes a pubescent girl's troubling relationship with her mother and her feelings of guilt for preferring her father at this time of her life; Modern Library, Westminster, Maryland.

For Men Only by Earnest Larsen; challenges society's definition of manliness, emphasizes the human qualities of a Christian man: sensitivity to others, reverence for sex, self-discipline; Liguori Publications, Liguori, Missouri.

From Parent to Child About Sex by Wilson W. Grant, M.D.; a blend of physiology facts and reverence for sex which readers can pass on to children.

Growing Up with Sex and *Living with Sex*, both by Richard F. Hettlinger; Seabury Press, New York.

Love, Sex and Being Human by Paul Bohannan; written especially for teenagers; Doubleday, Garden City, New York.

A Search for Meaning in Love, Sex and Marriage by Hugo L. Hurst; a valuable resource for parents in discussing sexuality in the language of the adolescent and the young adult; St. Mary's College Press, Winona, Minnesota.

Man and Woman by Ronald J. Wilkins; William Brown and Company, Dubuque, Iowa.

Parents and Home Sex Education by Gordon J. Lester; The Inland Register, Spokane, Washington.

P.E.T.: Parent Effectiveness Training by Thomas Gordon; training for parenthood; tested ways to rear happy children; Peter H. Wyden, Inc., New York.

Sex Education for the Developmentally Disabled by Fischer, Krajicek, and Borthick; designed for teaching retarded children; University Park Press, Baltimore, Maryland.

Sex and the Young Catholic by Gregory Kenny; Claretian Publications, Notre Dame, Indiana.

The Stork Is Dead by Charlie Shedd; a readable book, particularly good for middle to older teens; combines openness with a Christian perspective; Word Books, Waco, Texas.

What a Modern Catholic Believes About Sex and Marriage by Eugene Kennedy; Thomas More Press, Chicago.

What To Tell Your Child About Sex by the Child Study Association; this is a handy reference manual in paperback; offers typical questions from children and possible parent answers; Child Study Association, 9 East 89th St., New York 10028.

What Your Child Really Wants to Know About Sex and Why by Dr. William Block; Fawcett World, Greenwich, Connecticut.

CHAPTER 6

"Read It Again, Mom."
Fostering Values
Through Literature

He was late walking. He was late talking. All the other kids in the neighborhood rode trikes before he did. He caught up, but he was always the last one in the group to achieve the normal. He sensed his parents' anxiety, as children always do, and he tried harder, but it just discouraged him.

Then one day his mother bought him a book: *Leo the Late Bloomer* by Robert Kraus (Windmill Books, Inc.). It became his bible. "Read it to me," he demanded daily, and his parents did. This delightful story of Leo, a young lion who doesn't bloom as early as his friends, became his solace. It calmed the boy's fears that he wasn't as good as the other children, and it helped his parents understand the depth of his feelings.

"A simple five-dollar book did what dozens of visits to the pediatrician couldn't do," said his father. "It showed him he wasn't alone in his problem and gave him hope that he would bloom someday, too."

Teaching values through literature isn't new. On the contrary, it's probably the oldest teaching method used by humans. From Old Testament stories through *Pilgrim's Progress* to Horatio Alger, cultures have used this method to inculcate prevailing morals and values.

A friend of mine who had never taught bowed to the urgings of her pastor to "try her hand" at a CCD class. She called me in despair. "The kids are nice enough," she said, "but they're zombies. Nothing I do interests them. Will you come over and tell me what I'm doing wrong, please?"

47

I did. She wasn't doing anything wrong, really, except boring the children to despair. Nobody could have been interested in the materials she was using. Her CCD budget was miniscule, and she didn't have the professional teaching know-how to create materials of her own.

So there we were with a non-teacher, a non-budget, and twenty-two second graders coming in from schools filled with resource centers, reading machines, and libraries bulging with colorful books.

We were searching for the miracle to catch and keep the interest of these eight-year-olds long enough to teach them some religious traditions and values. We found the miracle in the public library, right there on the shelves ignored by television-sated youngsters whose parents don't read to them anymore because there's never time.

We began with dinosaurs. They mesh beautifully with Genesis, and no second grader can *not* get caught up with the saga of dinosaurs. It's not in his nature, or her nature, either. Dinosaurs appeal to every child from four to ten. The names parents find difficult to pronounce—brontosaurus, triceratops, and tyrannosaurus rex—roll easily off the tongues of delighted youngsters.

There's something about the dinosaur era that catches the youngster's imagination, and it's not just the size of the animals. I think that children respond to very deep feelings inside of them when pondering dinosaurs: Who made them, how long ago did they roam the earth, how could they (or, indeed, anything) precede me, why did they disappear, and could I, too, disappear as a species?

It's foolish to think that children are going to articulate such feelings and questions. They probably don't even know they have them, but if we use something as attractive as the dinosaur and other stories to allow questions to surface, we'll find ourselves dealing with deep moral questions on their level, and without the aid of a religion text. My friend used the unit to explore the contradictory school-Church stories on how the world began, leading the young ones to the idea that they need not be contradictory but can be complementary. She followed it with the all-consuming question to children, "What happened to the dinosaurs?" Were they destroyed by the ice age? Will there be another ice age? She read about Noah and the flood and God's promise never to flood the earth again.

Did smaller animals eat the eggs of the dinosaurs, thus forcing extinction? A wonderful moral to young children is the one that might doesn't make security. She used David and Goliath here.

My friend's teaching problem changed. "How can I get away from dinosaurs?" she asked. We proceeded to map out a year's plan for teaching religion through children's literature, and it proved quite popular.

I think parents, moreso than teachers, ignore a most valuable tool in rearing their children with good moral values when they bypass children's literature. Because the books aren't labeled "religious" or "Catholic," many parents presume they're just story books for entertainment. Yet once these same parents become familiar with both the book and the process of reading it with the child, they become devoted primary religious educators through literature.

Once a parent has read aloud *The Velveteen Rabbit* to his or her child, the idea of parent love and God's love will be forever changed. "You can't be ugly, except to people who don't understand," explains the Skin Horse. And to children who have loved special toy animals, his words on becoming real are profound: "Generally, by the time you are Real, most of your hair has been loved off, and your eyes drop out and you get loose in the joints and very shabby."

The aging process and the resurrection ending prepare the children for later teaching of truths which they can't understand now but which they can experience on an elementary level. Parents don't have to elaborate on the theme. The children understand it. Chances are they already felt the lesson with their own stuffed animals, but the beauty of the story lies in having it experienced by another who was perceptive enough to write it down.

I used *The Velveteen Rabbit* once in a parents' workshop for a Valentine's Day demonstration paraliturgy on love. The parents' reaction was heartwarming. "Why didn't I ever hear that story before? I can't wait to read it to my children," and the inevitable "Where can I get the book?"

We haven't been made aware of the hundreds of Velveteen Rabbits available to us. If we aren't teachers or children's writers, we aren't expected to become experts in this most valuable of parent resources. But I strongly recommend that parishes include as part of their family education program annual workshops or evenings on children's literature. If the parish personnel feel inadequate in offering them, they can engage the local children's librarian, a bookshop owner, or any primary teacher to come in and discuss children's books with values: what they are, where to obtain them, and how to use them. Such a workshop or evening is an excellent time to present a book fair. If parishes invite a local or nearby metropolitan bookstore to set up displays of books with values and make them available, parents will buy them.

Once they've invested their money, they'll invest the time to read them to their children. Once they experience their children's reactions, they're apt to continue. As reading specialist Nancy Larrick writes:

> When you have read aloud to a child a great deal, you will understand what delight it gives him. And, if you are completely honest, you will admit you have enjoyed it just about as much. Few activities create a warmer relationship between child and grownup than reading aloud. It is deeply flattering to be read to and have the undivided attention of an adult. And for the adult, there is great satisfaction in sharing a child's absorption in words and pictures.

If parishes budgeted a mere hundred dollars annually for building up a lending library of books with values, this would be educational money better spent than had it been used on religious workbooks that are discarded yearly. Included in the order should be several copies of Nancy Larrick's *A Parent's Guide to Children's Reading,* from which I just quoted.

So popular has been this book that it's in its fourth edition, and its sections on "Books They Like" (age and interest indexed), "Building a Home Library," and "Who Am I? What Do I Value?" alone make it worth $1.95. In addition, author Larrick covers children of television—their reading habits and needs—, poetry, children's book clubs, and, in a short chapter, "Don't Be Afraid," she encourages parents to allow and even introduce their adolescents to literature dwelling on real-life problems of today.

She writes:

Such books as *The Outsider, Durango Street, Soul Brothers and Sister Lou,* and *Lions in the Way* are a new experience to most of the teachers I meet. I suspect that very few parents have read them—or even looked at them. Although young people are turning more and more to books written for adults, it is a rare adult who reads a contemporary juvenile novel. That is one reason why the generation gap has become an unnecessary chasm.

I nearly cheered at that paragraph. My personal experience bears out her words. As an ex-English teacher turned-mother-turned-writer, I have always put books in front of my children. Now my teenager is putting books in front of me. "Read that, will you, Mom? I think you'll like it," she said once as she handed me *The Outsiders.*

Well, I didn't like it at all. I thought it shallow, exaggerated, and poorly characterized. It was a story told from the viewpoint of lonely teenagers living without adults while blaming them for their inadequacies and using violence to find a kind of companionship. But my critical opinion wasn't as important as the question, Why did my daughter like it, and why did she want me to read it?

She was attracted by the loneliness of the young people and their unorthodox concern for one another. My defensiveness evaporated when I realized she wanted me to read it not because it zapped parents but because she really thought I'd like it and she wanted to discuss the teenagers' actions with me.

Likewise, my eleven-year-old son, after telling me the whole story page by page as he read it, now wants me to read *The Prince of Central Park* by Evan H. Rhodes. This paperback deals with a boy who, beaten by his foster mother, runs off and builds a tree house in Central Park. I am going to read it because some messages in that book appeal strongly to Mike, and he wants to share them. It may help me know him better.

I would like to see adult discussion clubs in parishes built around a year of reading juvenile literature, particularly popular pre-teen and teen literature. Why do youth like *Are You There, God? It's Me Margaret* and *The Pigman* and *The Outsiders* so well? What can parents learn about themselves and their children by reading these books—most of which take only an evening? Mrs. Larrick sums up her chapter with this paragraph:

> You can begin at home to introduce such books and to initiate the kind of open-question discussion which will bring out children's experiences and possibly their anxieties. Fiction and nonfiction about sex, divorce, desertion, drugs, street gangs, poverty, pollution, and war may seem bitter fare for the youngster you still think of as your baby. But these are subjects he gets on television, the people and scenes he meets as he walks down the street. Suitable or not, this is life today in the United States. Don't be afraid to discuss the books that can help to make that life more significant for your child.

We are the most reading-conscious nation in the world. We spend millions of dollars annually trying to improve children's reading ability, yet we don't go beyond reading as a skill. As long as our children know how to read, we aren't concerned that they don't read.

I'm not going to go into a tirade against television. It has a potential we haven't tapped, along with a power that often frightens us as parents. Whatever else, it has changed our nation's reading habits. Deep values can't be inculcated in an hour's show. Characterizations, solutions, and values tend to remain superficial rather than internalized as they are in the reading experience.

That's why children who have read books like *Winnie the Pooh, Charlotte's Web* and Felix Salter's *Bambi* feel cheated when they see them on television. Oh, they like the animation and visual appeal, but at the end they're apt to express a disappointed "But that wasn't what really happened," or "That was a kind of make-believe Charlotte." They sense the difference between sustained and repeated values and glimpsed ones.

Can television and literature coexist in the American home today? Yes, but it takes effort. It requires that parents be familiar with good children's literature and that they be willing to share it with their children. Weekly trips to the library can become as valuable as weekly CCD classes if parents are conscientious about helping children choose books and then read them with them. I'm astonished at how many parents have never gone to the library with their children. Reading parents beget reading children. Both beget discussing families—a rare commodity today.

If children have special problems like lying or feeling unloved, unattractive, or friendless, parents can ask librarians for suggested books on the problem. Libraries have bibliographies and source books that deal with special problems and values.

I know a school psychologist who begins counseling youngsters by reading with them *Where the Wild Things Are* by Maurice Sendak. "It gives me credibility," she said. "They know I'm going to allow them to express their feelings." This fine little book about a boy's temper tantrum and his ultimate return to forgiveness shows children that others sometimes share their confusing feelings. The psychologist begins each session with ten minutes of reading, quieting the children and taking them out of themselves and their world to view their actions from the perspective of fiction.

These sources are available to all of us, not just to teachers, psychologists, and moralists. They belong to us and should be counted as family treasures. In a society searching for values, we seem to be overlooking a valuable triad: parental time, children's stories, and the eternal suspense of what's going to happen on the next page.

A Family Shelf of Books With Values
by Dolores Curran

A Certain Small Shepherd by Rebecca Caudill; family; about Christmas
All About Dinosaurs by Roy Chapman Andrews; family
Any good book of Mother Goose
Any good fairy tale collection
Are You My Mother? by P.D. Eastman; 2-6
Are You There, God? It's Me, Margaret by Judy Blume; 10-12
Bambi by Felix Salter; family
The Beech Tree by Pearl Buck; family; on aging
Bible Stories Retold by David Kossoff
Boxcar Children, The by Gertrude Chandler Warner; 8-10
Brighty of the Grand Canyon by Marguerite Henry; 9-12
Carrot Seed, The by Ruth Krauss; 2-6
Charlotte's Web by E.B. White; family
Diary of a Young Girl by Anne Frank; adolescent
Free to Be . . . You and Me by Marlo Thomas et. al.; family
Giving Tree, The by Shel Silverstein
Grandfather and I by Helen E. Buckley; 2-7
Heidi by Johanna Spyri; family
Hope for the Flowers by Trina Paulus; family
Horse in Harry's Room, The by Syd Hoff; 2-6
Ira Sleeps Over by Bernard Waber; 4-8
Leo the Late Bloomer by Robert Kraus; 6-8
Little Bear, The (series) by Else Holmelund; 6-8
Little House, The (series) by Laura Ingalls Wilder; family
Little Women by Louisa May Alcott; family
Man of the House, The by Joan Fassler; 5-8
My Grandpa Died Today by Joan Fassler; family
Nobody Listens to Andrew by Elizabeth Guilfoile; 4-8
Owls in the Family by Farley Mowat; family
Prayers from the Ark by Carmen De Gastztold; family
Quarreling Book, The by Charlotte Zolotow; family reconciliation
Ramona the Pest by Beverly Cleary; 5-8; little sisters
Rascal by Sterling North; 9-11; also family
Sounder by William H. Armstrong; family

CHAPTER 7

Prayer and Celebration in the Future Shock Family

Once I heard a terrific argument between parents on whether children should learn memorized prayers or learn how to pray spontaneously. Frankly, neither parent made much sense, but the final rejoinder came from a mother who said emphatically, "It doesn't matter if the child doesn't understand the prayers. If God understands them, that's all that counts."

I decided then and there to write on prayer. And I pray I don't merely add to the confusion that already abounds in many minds, especially those of children, over the purpose and manner of prayer.

Many parents from my generation worry because their children don't know their prayers. They wonder why the Church isn't teaching them anymore. At the same time, the Church wonders why families aren't saying them anymore.

The question seems to come down to which is better, memorized prayer or spontaneous prayer. Both have a purpose and both have drawbacks. The most obvious drawback to memorized prayer is that children don't always know what they're saying.

One youngster explained earnestly that prayer words were hard words because only God was supposed to know what they meant. Our Catholic magazines are full of "humorous" anecdotes about children's misunderstanding of prayers; e.g., "He suffered under a bunch of violets."

For building an intimate relationship with God—being able to really talk with him—memorized prayer isn't that valuable to children. But memorized prayers have the intrinsic value of being there when children grow up to need them.

When they're older and can understand them, they can reach back into their childhood and find the words they didn't understand then. This is the real value of most memory work: the basics, such as math tables and geographic places, are there to be used later when the concepts are better understood.

That's why I think it's important that a child learn some prayers. In our family we stress the Our Father, Hail Mary, and Act of Contrition. It's futile to teach post-Vatican II children the Apostles' Creed because they get it all confused with the Creed at Mass, a problem we didn't have because our childhood Mass creed was in Latin.

Although we teach prayers, spontaneous prayer is much more important than memorized prayers in our home. I think it's far sadder to see an adult who can't pray spontaneously than a child who hasn't learned his or her prayers. Many of today's adults become acutely uncomfortable at spontaneous prayer. They grew up in a Church of formulized prayer, and anything else seems foreign and a little sacrilegious.

Yet there is a thirst for a personal spirituality today, and we're finding adults flocking to charismatic groups where they feel free to pray openly and joyously. Similarly, young people are joining campus Jesus groups which foster spontaneous prayer and Scripture discussion.

Prayer doesn't have to be an either/or proposition. Let's teach our children the prayers we want them to reach for some day and ask our parish for help in teaching our children, and ourselves, to pray spontaneously as well.

"A hurried prayer is no prayer at all."

This bit of wisdom from the Green Bay book, *Prayer: Family Style*, sums it up for many of today's families. We want to pray more, and we want to learn to pray openly together, but when?

Not on Monday nights because there's basketball practice. Tuesday nights are out—Dad's late night at the office—and so on. Even the most sincere family gets frustrated trying to find a half hour to talk to God together quietly and unrushed.

How can we go about finding time for prayer in the Future Shock family? I suggest that families start with two simple occasions: grace at meals and prayers in the car. Instead of "Bless us, O Lord," take advantage of this minute of family prayer time daily to sneak into spontaneous prayer.

Join hands and sing "The Great Amen" from *Lilies of the Field* for starters. A week later, sing a short response from Mass. "Glory to God, glory, O praise him, alleluia," is a good one. Work your way up to any of the songs you enjoy from Mass.

Once you're able to break the "Bless us, O Lord" barrier with song, you'll be able to do it with words of your own. A parent can begin by saying a spontaneous grace such as "Thank you, God, that all went well at school, work, and home today. Thanks for this good lasagne and bring us closer to you tomorrow. Amen."

These aren't "church words" but family words, and because they are familiar ones, children are more apt to use them when their chance at homemade grace comes. Let the parents alternate for awhile, and then open it up to the children.

Eventually, try a short grace around the table where each family member offers a prayer similar to the ones at Mass: "That I'll pass the algebra test tomorrow, let us pray" ... "Lord, hear our prayer."

Car prayer can also be effective. We always say a rosary early in the morning on the days we travel. It was on these trips that the children learned the various mysteries and asked questions about them. If parents don't adhere to the rosary format too rigidly, children in the car like to hear stories before each decade, such as the one of Simeon in the temple recognizing the divinity of the Babe.

When you are traveling long distances, you have lots

of time to while away, and you aren't interrupted by phone or oven buzzer. The children, too, can ask question after question, without being told, "Not now, I'm too busy."

For families who find the above too uncomfortable, try having the children, and parents, write out little prayers for special occasions and read them at mealtime or bedtime. This is often a more effective way for the family new to such activity to slip into the habit of family prayer.

And a habit it is. Remember that prayer in the family isn't a gift, nor does it require special talents. All it takes is time and repetition until you all become familiar enough with it to be comfortable. Then you have to worry about its becoming too casual. But that's another problem, hopefully a long way off.

Preparing for the Sacraments—Together

"Just exactly why does the Church want us to prepare our children for First Communion?" writes a thoughtful mother. "It doesn't teach us anything we don't already know. It surely isn't the most efficient use of personnel—teaching parents to teach children instead of teaching children directly. It's terribly difficult to fit lessons into a busy family's schedule, and there's no certainty that the child is prepared when parents do it.

"I suspect it's to lure parents to classes through their children. Is that right?"

No, it isn't right, but this woman has touched on a lot of unspoken parental things that need airing. I don't think we've done a good job of explaining just exactly why we want parents involved in their children's sacramental preparations. It isn't because there's a nun shortage, although I frequently hear parents express that suspicion, and it isn't to lure parents back to classes, although that's a welcome bonus.

The main reason is much simpler: *to force parents and child to spend some time together on God.* That's not theological language, I know. I could use phrases like "a quality of spiritual relationship," but parents have heard those and still don't understand "just exactly why." So, in honest parent language, let me explain.

We parents spend very little quiet time alone with each child. Three hundred eighth-grade boys kept a log on father-son time in a two-week period. The average father and son spent seven and a half minutes a week alone together. In this time, we expect the relationship to cover problems of growing up, school, cars, ideas, values, and religion.

Only a fraction of the already-little quiet time we spend with an individual child is spent on anything remotely resembling religious belief. God doesn't get on the family calendar unless he's scheduled in. He's usually scheduled for Sunday morning and Tuesday afternoon CCD, both away from home and in the church where, according to many parents, he belongs.

Thus, children grow up—as did their parents—believing that God lives in church, not in people. Just as many seven-year-olds still believe that doctors live in hospitals and teachers live at school, they identify God with a church building.

At this age it's crucial to their faith development to identify God with their parents. Yet parents consistently fight involvement. They see their role as having the children and thereafter having them at the right place at the right time to get religion.

So few parents ever discuss God, morals, or values with their children that we literally have to force them to do so. Otherwise, children rightly believe that it isn't interesting enough or important enough to talk about. "Go ask Sister " or "Because Father says so" isn't adequate theology for this generation, a generation that already suspects religion is more a cultural than a committed thing in their parents' lives.

What confuses children is that parents tell them religion is important. If it's important, they don't have to be told. They know by the amount of enthusiasm their parents show and the amount of time their parents spend on it if it's important. The only time many parents spend on their children's religious nourishment comes in driving them to CCD class.

That's why we want parental involvement in sacramental preparation. It might be the only time the child and parent really discuss God together in their entire family life. And every child deserves that experience once or twice before he or she leaves home.

Sometime during this year, hundreds of you will attend parish sessions on how to prepare your child for the sacraments. You'll be given the vital three M's: motivation, methods, and materials, and you should come home with a fair idea of what to do.

However, some will find the experience more rewarding than others. I'd like to offer a fourth M, miscellany, with some do's and don't's for parents once they get home.

Don't approach the lessons as "have to's" but as "get to's." You may find the lessons inconvenient, but your child enjoys any time alone with Mom and Dad. Remember the boy who liked being sick because "My mom comes in and sits on my bed and we just talk"? If you give the impression that the lessons are interrupting your free time, the child will feel guilty and negative about them.

Do seek a spot where you won't be interrupted. One that is conducive to reading and discussion rather than activity and distraction. Give your child a break every so often to get the handsprings out of his or her system.

Don't call the child away from TV or play to have your session. Effective parent-preparers tell me they schedule sessions ahead of time with their youngsters and unless something important comes up, they stick to it. This allows the child a voice in the planning and reminds parents to prepare.

Do consider that there are two parents in most families. Mom alone isn't responsible for the children's faith, although our culture has assigned her to that role. Active participation by Dad in sacramental preparation will do a lot to kill that notion.

Don't be bound by the book. Remember that you know the child better than the book does. Use the book, but if you want to stray from it to use a library book or tell a story to make a point, do so. If your child is fascinated by some offshoot, such as persecution of early Christians, take time to discuss it.

Do understand you're creating a bond your child will treasure. Many tales have been written by famous adults recalling pleasant memories of learning with their parents. Although many didn't understand it all at the time, they cherished the time their parents spent with them in sharing religious belief. In our television-centered homes, this time is even more precious.

Don't worry about hurting your child. Children have to understand very little in order to receive First Communion. They have to distinguish between ordinary bread and consecrated bread and have to have a desire to receive. They need to understand the miracle that Jesus *is* the host, but they can't possibly understand the theology of transubstantiation. Some parents worry so much about underteaching that they overteach, and then they find sacramental preparation distasteful instead of pleasant.

Do help the child plan his or her First Communion day. Make it a special family day, perhaps with a picnic or a family dinner to which grandparents and godparents are invited. Use part of your lessons to design place mats, banners, and invitations. This injects the idea that the lessons lead up to a joyous event rather than to relief when the whole thing is over.

Let's Bring Back the Saints

I was delighted to read an article in *Living Light* by Father
Berard Marthaler of Catholic University on the need to bring
the saints back into religious education. He says: "Just
as patriotic figures express the ideals of a nation,
so saintly Christians embody the ideals and values of the
Church. From the very beginning of the Church, the
example of gifted Christians has played a formative role in
the Christian education of the young and old alike."

Those of us educated in an olden-days style of
catechism remember as the brightest parts of religion class
Bible history and the lives of the saints. I can attest from
experience with today's children that they react similarly.
They love to hear stories of persecutions, of courage, of
goodness, and of counter-culture Christians throughout the
ages, and many of our saints *were* the counter-culture of
their day. (G. K. Chesterton quipped, "It is the paradox of
history that each generation is converted by the saint who
contradicts it most.")

Father Marthaler explained that the scholars who
purged Christopher and Philomena from the official
collection didn't intend "to write a modern chapter in
iconoclasm but to bring the saints back to life, to rescue
them from the plaster-of-paris molds that robbed them of
their individuality and identity. In sum, the saints have
probably suffered more at the hands of their friends than
their enemies."

It's unfortunate that the move to purge the calendar
of the non-existent saints and the admission of retouching
saints' biographies to make them less human came in the
wake of Vatican II. Many Catholics felt the Church was
throwing out the saints. That was never intended.

I'm sorry that many of our children don't know
anything about saints, some not even about their patron
saints. In our own family, we try to celebrate an annual
saint's nameday for each of us, parents included. (At mine,
I'm always reminded that Dolores means pains!) Once we
even had a parish nameday festival where each family had a

booth (cardtable) with symbols, statues, and other paraphernalia surrounding the patron saints in their family.

Family by family, we introduced ourselves as our saints and gave a capsule biography. The listeners were fascinated because the lives of the saints are fascinating. I suggest it as an idea for religious television, if it ever gets underway.

Good books on the saints have been rare lately, but three paperbacks for the family library are worth mentioning. One I wouldn't be without is *My Nameday: Come for Dessert* by Helen McLoughlin (The Liturgical Press). It gives short biographies of the major saints, their feast day, symbol, decorations, and recipes. Phyllis McGinley's *Saint-Watching* (Doubleday, $1.75) is fun to read and particularly useful in a family of older children. The third is a new pair called *Saint of the Day*, volumes I and II (St. Anthony Messenger Press). Edited by Leonard Foley, O.F.M., this set includes a life and lesson for each of the 173 saints in the New Missal. (Brace yourself, parents. Out of 173, two are listed as parents and one as husband.)

Winston Press has a new series for children: Stories About Christian Heroes. Each book in the series is a story dealing with a significant event in the life of a well-known Christian man or woman. The series includes stories about Elizabeth Seton, John Neumann, Francis of Assisi, Martin de Porres, Elizabeth Fry, and Queen Margaret of Scotland.

I suggest that teachers use the saints to involve the families. Ask each family to delve into parish-supplied books and tell each child the story of his or her patron. Follow this with a pageant or program in which the children act out brief sketches of their saints' lives. Have the children make patron saint scrapbooks, working either individually with their families, or in a class group. Or have a class patron saint Mass—anything to restore the saints to their place in our children's lives.

After the Turkey, Before the Game

Want to try something a little different on Thanksgiving? Give your family or class something besides turkey and football? How about an honest-to-goodness Walton-sort of down-home giving of thanks?

Before you write this off as one of those "Advent wreath" chapters, reflect with me a minute on why we Catholics find it so hard to say more than a perfunctory grace on the day we set aside to give thanks. Thanksgiving has never been big with Catholics, probably because it didn't even appear on our liturgical or holy calendars until a decade ago. Prior to that it was considered a Protestant or national rather than Catholic holiday.

Happily that has changed, but we inherit our past and still find it uncomfortable to direct spontaneous family prayers together. Add to this our custom of inviting others to share the Thanksgiving meal with us, plus the inevitable football games which determine the time and length of our feast, and we seem to have a challenge on our hands.

Yet Thanksgiving is one of the most natural of feast days. Next to Christmas, it is the one most easily understood by children, and it's an ideal time to start families on a prayer-and-celebration track.

If you're a teacher, suggest some of these activities to your students and encourage them to take them home to use for Thanksgiving. If you're a parent, pick and choose those that appeal.

Choose a time of relaxation, preferably at the end of the meal. I know the old home-liturgy books used to encourage spontaneous thanks at the beginning of holiday meals, but maybe that's why nobody practiced them. The beginning is always rushed, with Mom getting food on while it's still hot, and the children so hungry they can't concentrate on anything but growling stomachs.

At the close of the meal, light a special candle or two, begin with any appropriate hymn—"What a Great Thing It Is," "Joy Is Like the Rain," or "God the Father, Hear Our Prayer" are just a few—, and use one or more of the suggested homemade prayers of thanksgiving listed below.

One of the keys to success is to prepare the day or the week before. A CCD teacher might have the students do the litany or the special prayers in class and then take them home. Parents can complement the teacher by doing the same "assignment" themselves.

Suggested Homemade Prayers of Thanksgiving

1. Write a litany of thanksgiving for your family, having each member responsible for ten items. One person can read the litany with the others responding; e.g., "For helping me find a part-time job," (response) "We give you thanks, O Lord."
2. Use John Denver's song, "Hey, It's Good to Be Back Home Again," and follow with homemade verses to fit the family; especially good for families with teenagers.
3. Ask each family member to offer an original prayer of thanks which includes: a) the persons, places, and events of the past year for which they are most thankful, b) the things that didn't happen, for which they are thankful, and c) a prayer of hope for the upcoming year.
4. Instead of linen, use a paper cloth and have the family draw designs and graffiti of thanks and share them.
5. Go around the table and ask each member to choose an individual or a group of people for whom they feel a special affinity: "For those who are lonely," "For those in pain," "For those who are hungry." Each person can be encouraged to explain why he or she feels close to a certain group in need and give concrete ways he or she can help in the coming year to relieve that need so "his" or "her" people will have more to be thankful for next Thanksgiving.

Advent, Christmas, Lent, and Holy Week

No Time at the Inn

If Jesus were born in our culture, I'm sure we'd find lots of room for him at the inns, but I'm not so sure we'd find time for him. As a matter of fact, many of us don't find time for him during the whole holiday season, a season, incidentally, that's beginning to span a two-month period.

Today's family finds time an ever-more-precious commodity, and many parents, sincere about spending more time with their children, perceive the irony of being too busy with family activities to actually spend time with the family. Many a dad wonders what he's doing at a Cub Scout board meeting when he'd rather be home with his sons.

Many parents appreciate the irony of hearing how they should spend more time with their children, during a meeting scheduled by school or church, which takes them away from their families for another evening.

In truth, some parents are so busy learning how to be good parents they become absent parents. Whenever I give a workshop for parents, I advise them not to attend another meeting or workshop on family religious enrichment until they've actually had time to show results in the home from their previous meeting.

Still, the time problem is real. "We can hardly find time to eat together," remarks a mother. "How will we find time to celebrate as a family?"

Since we're not going to create more time, our only alternative is to enhance the quality of time spent with our families. In the Advent season this means creative approaches to restoring a religious dimension to our secularized activities.

For instance, a family can create a paraliturgy around decorating the tree, addressing cards, wrapping packages, baking cookies, and other activities, which can be a headache if done alone by Mom. Nobody stole the spirituality of the holidays from us. We gave it away by putting labels on our festivities: Advent wreaths are religious but Christmas trees aren't; "Noel" is holy but "Deck the Halls" isn't.

I'm reminded of a cartoon by Doug Brunner, who has a character agonizing, "Of all the holidays, I have the most difficulty with Christmas. I was brought up with Santa and Jesus, the Church and tinsel. What Christmas do you celebrate?"

His friend replies, "I alternate."

That's what most of us do. We alternate. We attend a prayer meeting before a cocktail party. We decorate the tree and then put up the crib. We buy gifts and Christmas seals.

We don't stop our frenzy long enough to realize that those nostalgic things we label religious were the secular practices of another age. Many were traditions from a culture that practiced one faith and one set of traditions. There was no sharp distinction between the sacred and the secular. The Christmas tree, for example, which we consider a secular observance of Christmas, was considered part of the sacred festivities surrounding Christmas in the "old country," simply because it was used to enrich Christmas.

Because we tend to separate the two, we read our more dualistic view back into old customs, then feel apologetic about our "secular" practices.

To return to a believable observance of Christmas, we have to stop considering our "secular" traditions atheistic and start recognizing their religious possibilities. If this means working the *Nutcracker Suite* or even Rudolph into a religious framework, so be it. It can be done.

Those who cringe at this idea as "sacrilegious" should recall that our ancestors used almost any occasion to celebrate God: blessing fields, collecting harvest, even cleaning house in the spring.

What Was It All About, Mom?

One problem with our Christmas observance is the tremendous sense of letdown when the whole thing ends. We get so caught up in the activity of the moment, be it school program or TV special, that we keep postponing the depth of the celebration.

Many Catholic families know more about the Grinch than the Wise Men. Few have time to develop cherishable family traditions for their children to pass on to their own families when they leave home. No wonder one theologian calls our holiday season "our annual winter festival" rather than a religious holiday.

Our lives become fragmented into a series of events—"religious" and "secular," Church, school, and home. Let's try to bring these fragments together and discover how they relate to each other and to the central event of Jesus' birth.

Let's remember, too, that our Advent preparations lead us *into* Christmas. Our celebration of the Birth should not end with it but continue through at least until Epiphany. The suggestions that follow will help avoid the December 26 letdown and enrich our sense of the spiritual meaning of Christmas at the same time. Read these ideas together. Choose any that seem to fit your family, or create your own and set about accomplishing them before it's January 6 and the kids ask, "Is that all there is, Dad? What was it all about, Mom?"

Christmas-card liturgy Instead of having Mom feel sorry for herself sitting alone doing cards, put the family around the table. As Mom and Dad address cards, children can stuff, seal, and stamp them. Or the family can make its own cards, giving each person the opportunity to design one or two "originals." This is the *time together* that TV steals from us, time that is important in developing rich family relationships.

While card work is going on, an older child or a parent can read the nativity story from Luke's Gospel, selections from Dickens' *Christmas Carol*, or a little Christmas story. Follow this with carols, and stop to talk of friends and relatives when one of the children asks, "Who's Mabel Anderson?"

Beginning the card liturgy with a prayer and ending it with that old standby, dimming lights, holding hands, and singing the "Our Father," will add all the "holiness" we need to a formerly secular event.

Decorating-the-tree liturgy This is essentially the same as the card liturgy, but preface it with a prayer like this: "Our Father, who gives us trees and all beautiful things, thank you for our tree. Help us to decorate it in excitement and joy in anticipation of your Son's coming. Lead us not onto each other's toes but give us the blessing of realizing how lucky we are to have one another, a tree, and you. Amen." Sing Amen together and start decorating.

Stop occasionally to sit back, admire your work, have a sip of eggnog, and enjoy the time *together* that the holiday steals from us. End with a prayer and a song. Chances are you will relive the same celebration years from now when you visit your grandchildren at Christmas, because our children are thirsty for religious traditions to hold on to and pass on.

The above format can also be used for a Package-wrapping liturgy, a Cookie-baking liturgy, a Getting-the-house-ready-for-Grandma liturgy, and liturgies for the myriad of other traditions that we used to look upon as chores rather than as opportunities during the season.

The Jesse Tree   One drawback I run into in encouraging families to celebrate is their past dismal experience with an Advent ceremony. "Ohhh," parents groan, "don't mention Advent to us. We tried that and it was a dud."

Catholic families have reason to feel this way. Most of the prayers we were encouraged to say around the wreath were stilted, awkward, and incomprehensible to children. That has changed today, but the experience lingers, and many families refuse to give it another try.

I like the Jesse tree better. It's a much richer liturgy, loaded with possibilities, and can include the Advent wreath and family crib (creche) traditions. In my experience children relate to it well.

Basically, the Jesse tree is the family tree of Jesus. It celebrates the great ones who waited: from Adam to Noah to Jonah. In one of the best family celebration aids, a book called, *Come Out!* (World Library Publications, 2145 Central Parkway, Cincinnati, Ohio 45214), there are patterns for Jesse Tree ornaments and a simple ceremony. I strongly recommend this book for all kinds of occasions because it is so workable in today's family.

But it isn't necessary to have a book. You need a tree of some sort; a dead branch will do, or a large felt tree hanging, or a poster-board cutout. Finding or constructing the tree is a good job for one child. A teenager can fashion a tree from plywood.

Have a family evening drawing and cutting out Jesse symbols. Here are some: Jacob's ladder, Joseph's coat, Noah's ark, David's harp. Use your family imagination on designs and materials. They can be drawn and colored, made of felt, clay, or even woodburned.

Start any time. It doesn't have to be the first Sunday in Advent. For your evening ceremony, light the candles, sing a carol, read a religious holiday story (the little Arch books are good for this use). Then one child each evening presents his or her symbol and tells the story of its owner—for example, David or Noah. See what an opportunity this is to work in some Bible history? (And remember how much you enjoyed Bible history?) Hang the symbol on the tree. In our family we review all the hanging symbols each evening, and each child tries to outdo the other in recognizing them all.

Close out this simple ceremony by choosing a crib piece. The first night, set up the crib itself. Each succeeding night, have the youngest child reach into the box and choose a crib piece (be sure you have removed the Infant) and place it in the crib. By Christmas Eve, the crib should be ready for the Infant, and you can slip that into the manger just before your Christmas Eve Jesse-Advent liturgy. Be sure to set the Wise Men a distance away so they can be moved during the twelve days of Christmas until Epiphany.

The shine in your children's eyes, regardless of their age and sophistication, when the crib is full and the family is prepared both spiritually and emotionally for the Savior is worth all the effort you have put into it.

Additional suggestions to consider:
- Make your own Christmas cards.
- Hold a neighborhood caroling party.
- Write a Christmas letter to every close relative.
- Offer to shop for a homebound person or help him or her to create something.

- Build an outdoor crib from old materials.
- Draw angels in the snow (or sand, you warm ones).
- Have an evening Advent or caroling period.
- Have each member make a surprise gift for the whole family: a poster, a sand candle, a cake, a pillow, a prayer, a poem, a picture, a plant, a what's-it?
- At dessert read together for fifteen minutes portions of a Christmas story or Scripture.
- Visit a different church each week during Advent; afterward, visit a nursing home.
- Sculpt a snow Nativity scene.
- Choose individual windows or rooms to decorate.
- Brainstorm a Stations of the Crib and use it this year and next.
- Decorate the tree with homemade decorations only.
- Learn the words—all of them—of ten carols. Write some new verses.
- Put on a family/friends Christmas pageant.
- Have a birthday party for Jesus.
- Reconcile with someone.
- Make a holiday table cloth using old materials and new ideas.
- Turn out TV, lights, and music to tell stories under the tree.
- Ask Grandpa, Grandma, and other relatives what Christmas was like in the "olden days."
- Decorate cookies and deliver them, even the messy ones.
- Make up a Christmas Bingo or Monopoly game together, using events and personages of the season.
- Set aside a TV-less evening each week during Advent to get ready together spiritually.
- Send special Christmas letters to godparents.
- Make your own wrapping paper with crayons, felt pens, and grocery sacks.
- Take the family to the Sacrament of Reconciliation.
- Make a family banner for your home or parish.

- Plant a bulb or make some candy for those important adults in our lives: teachers, pastors, bus drivers.
- Make some luminaries out of brown paper sacks, sand, and candles; decorate the outside of them and light them on Christmas Eve.
- Start a neighborhood or parish *posada*. (Ask your Mexican-American friends about this lovely custom.)
- Build a bird feeder.
- Tape a letter and songs for faraway friends.
- Decorate a Christmas candle.
- Have family teenagers prepare Christmas morning breakfast or brunch.
- Make an outdoor Advent wreath or indoor wreaths of different materials.
- Have a family reconciliation service.
- Take a crisp family walk to hear the snow, the angels, and each other.
- Make a special little gift for the family for each of the Twelve Days of Christmas, ending January 6th.
- Move the Three Kings closer to the crib each of the twelve days and say a little family prayer during this simple liturgy.
- Have a family Epiphany party. Re-enact the coming of the Three Kings.

Lent—A Relic or a Reality?

"Let me tell you what Lent was like when I was little," begins Mom.

"Do we hafta listen?"

"Yes, you do," affirms Dad.

"Then will you talk fast so we can watch 'Mayhem in the Steets'? It starts in five minutes."

This version of family "lentness" is familiar to a lot of parents. It illustrates well the "We'll-work-it-in" attitude in modern families. The problem is we won't work it in and we know it. So we talk fast and give ourselves an outline of Lent rather than an experience of it.

Lent wasn't a perfect experience when we were young, but it was an experience, probably one of the best examples of experiential learning ever. We didn't learn about Lent as much as we lived it: we experienced sacrifice; we experienced hunger; we experienced personal spiritual scrutiny; we experienced prayer. We experienced the bleakness of Good Friday and, glory, we experienced the joy of Easter.

I doubt if many of today's children have really experienced any of that. We parents, so glib at criticizing the Church for abandoning Lent, abandoned it first in the home. That's where the child's daily experience is. If we parents don't want spiritually disadvantaged children, then we should offer them the experiences we found valid in yesteryear's Lent.

We don't have to wait for Rome to tell us to give up meat or Father to suggest we pray the rosary together. We are adults, in age if not in faith, and as such are spiritually responsible.

Remember last Good Friday when you said to yourself fervently, "Next year we're going to do something for Lent. I don't know how this Lent got away from us, but next year . . . . "

This is the next year you talked about last year and, knowing that my readers are trustworthy, I believe you. You really do want your family to do something during Lent, to experience Lent spiritually in some way, physically in some way, and intellectually in some way.

How can today's family work Lent into its busy schedule? Here is a list of suggestions for families. Adapt it to yours. If a weekly family Stations of the Cross isn't feasible because of the age of the children, then substitute Bible readings or prayers. Pick and choose from this list, but take the time to design a Lent suited to your family.

Then make a time commitment to Lent. It doesn't matter if it's only fifteen minutes a week; make the commitment. Put it on your calendar. And fulfill it.

Otherwise, this Good Friday you'll be saying, "Next year for *sure*, we're going to do something for Lent...."

Lenten suggestions
- Have a meatless day at home.
- Try reading the Bible for ten minutes at the end of dinner each day.
- Go without TV one day a week.
- Make a visit to a lonely old person or shut-in.
- Have weekly family Stations of the Cross.
- Say the family rosary.
- Hold weekly family lessons on Church history.
- Start Lent with an Ash Wednesday paraliturgy at home.
- How about daily Mass? A daily visit?
- Give up coffee and colas one day a week.
- Shovel walks for someone who can't.
- Volunteer to take the cancer envelope around.
- Go to the Sacrament of Reconciliation.
- Hold a family prayer session every Sunday night.
- Prepare for Holy Week with readings that lead up to Passover and the Last Supper.
- Undertake a weekly religion lesson with each child.
- Write a homemade family novena to Mary.
- Fast one complete day.
- Write a letter to someone who doesn't get many.
- No desserts; no snacks; no salt; no sugar; no smoking; no alcohol.
- Discuss your family's commitment to alleviating poverty.
- Teach the children the prayers you want them to know.
- Teach the family the old hymns you loved.
- Set aside one evening each week just for Lent.
- Have a home Mass.
- Listen to someone you don't enjoy.
- Walk one day instead of driving.
- Babysit for a mother who never gets out.
- Meditate ten minutes daily.

Or draw up your own list. Brainstorm it with your family, perhaps during a home Ash Wednesday observance. Ask each member to include: 1) a personal denial, 2) a family denial, 3) a personal spiritual commitment, 4) a family spiritual commitment, 5) a personal charitable commitment, 6) a family charitable commitment, and 7) a Lenten calendar. Get a large piece of poster paper or a three-ring notebook. Write down your commitments together. This is important because together you solidify your pledge to become more spiritual during the six weeks of Lent.

Once you have agreed on a family denial, such as no television on Wednesday nights, put it on the family's Lenten calendar. If one of the boys is going to drive an older person to Stations as part of his charitable commitment, schedule that. If little sister is going to read her children's Bible daily, put down when.

Add the big holy days of Lent, those which require more than a nod, like Holy Thursday and Good Friday, and talk about what the family can do to make them spiritually special.

In other words, let's experience Lent again. Let's not just talk about how it used to be. That puts the kiss of death on anything.

As long as we have memories and energy, we can re-create a Lenten experience in our families, and it can again become a living season, not a relic to be shelved with the dinosaur books.

A Family Holy Thursday Celebration

Explanation This is a combination Jewish paschal meal and Last Supper celebration and, as such, it's rich in heritage for Catholics. It's particularly appropriate for the family because it centers around a meal and doesn't require other guests.

Preparation During Lent read the story of the plagues leading up to the Exodus. The Golden Children's Bible has readable stories and pictures of the Pharaoh, Moses, and the plagues. Then as Holy Thursday approaches, each member of the family can do his or her part to prepare for the celebration.

The children paint red symbols on paper and hang them on the front door and in the dining room. These symbolize the blood of the paschal lamb which God instructed the Jews to paint on their doors so that the angel of death would "pass over" the home and not take the life of the firstborn son.

Mom prepares lamb and buys unleavened bread called matzo or matzos in the kosher section of the supermarket. Older children can even bake a simple unleavened bread to use.

One child prepares the Seder plate. On it are a sauce of bitter herbs (usually horseradish), which reminds the Jews of the bitterness of slavery; a hard-boiled egg and parsley as signs of spring; a roasted lamb bone (any bone will do) signifying the sacrifice, and charoset—a blend of chopped apples, nuts, and honey, symbolizing the mortar used in building the pyramids.

Set the table with a good cloth, dishes, and wine glasses.

Mother lights candles.

Celebration:

Dad: Tonight we celebrate the Passover when God said to Moses in Egypt: "Tell my people: every family must find a lamb. If a family is too small to eat a whole lamb, it should share a lamb with another family. The lamb must be young and without a mark on it. It may be either a goat or a sheep."

Child 1: "Slay the lamb and take some if its blood to put on the doorposts and lintels of every home of my people. That night they shall eat its roasted meat with bitter herbs and unleavened bread."

Child 2: "This is how you should eat it: with your sandals on and your staff in hand, like those in flight. It is the Passover of the Lord. On that same night I will send the angel of death through Egypt,

	striking down the firstborn of the land, both man and beast, punishing the gods of Egypt."
Child 3:	"But the lamb's blood on your houses will save you. I will pass over you; thus, when I strike the land of Egypt, nothing will hurt you. This day will be a great feast for you, which your children's children will celebrate."

Seder plate is passed and each item is explained. Family proceeds with meal. When finished, remove all but bread and wine.

Parent:	And so it was that before Passover, Jesus knew it was time for him to pass from earth to his father in heaven. And so, during supper, Jesus, leaving us himself as a new sacrifice, took the bread, broke it, and giving thanks said,
All:	"This is my body, which is for you. Do this in remembrance of me."
Parent:	And then he took some wine, poured it and said,
All:	"This cup is the new covenant in my blood. Drink this in memory of me."
Parent:	This bread and wine are but symbols of the holy sacrifice, and we recall that each year our ancestors celebrated as we are celebrating tonight, first the Passover and later the Last Supper on Holy Thursday.
Parent:	And each Sunday we rejoice that we share in the Body and Blood of Christ at Mass, which was begun tonight hundreds of years ago.

Each person takes some bread and wine. Candles are extinguished. All sing "This Is My Body" or some other suitable hymn.

Good Grief, It's Good Friday

If Good Friday creeps up unnoticed in your family, you still have time to initiate a profound paraliturgy without a lot of trouble. One that has been effective in many family groups is the modified Living Way of the Cross. It's best to have two or three families for this, so why not call friends and invite their families to join yours in this solemn holy day?

It's also good to have the children familiar with the

idea of the Way of the Cross before you undertake a family journey along it, so try to pray one or two prior to Good Friday.

As a basic format, set up the fourteen stations throughout your home. Some, like Stations Ten, Eleven, and Twelve, can be combined to save space. Adults or older children take the roles of Pontius Pilate, Simon, and Veronica, and the rest make the journey as Jesus. The leader can use any Way of the Cross pamphlet, but stay away from those with long texts.

We like three: *The Way of the Cross for Children* from Barton-Cotton, Inc., of Baltimore, *The Way of the Cross Today for Children* from Ave Maria Press, and the simple Way of the Cross from my old black *St. Joseph's Missal.*

Remember that children become restless easily, particularly if the role playing doesn't move along, and that they don't philosophize well when they're experiencing. It's the experience that we're stressing, the experience of walking the Way with Christ. If it's effective, each traveler will feel some of the loneliness, the fear, and the sacrifice of Christ. This is the essence of prayer.

Have each child or each family bring something: braided paper crowns of thorns, old sheets for robes, large paper crosses to pin on backs, Veronica's towel with a face sketched on it, soldiers' spears, and vinegar. Prior to the Way, have your children place large numbers throughout your home where a particular station will work best. If the weather is nice, have it outside. It lends more believability to the journey.

An adult places paper crowns of thorns on travelers' heads, another wraps them in robes, still another pins crosses on their backs at the appropriate time. One adult holds Veronica's towel and gently wipes each face as it passes. At Station Four, it's effective to have each mother act as Mary to her own children.

Without emphasizing the nailing and dying, which are too traumatic for young children, give each traveler a taste of vinegar on a cotton ball to experience the response to Jesus' thirst.

Some groups read the Seven Last Words at this time. Instead of having the travelers fall three times, I suggest genuflecting. Not only do twenty falling bodies make an unholy racket, but they also interrupt the spirit of the liturgy. A child who starts being silly should be politely asked to sit it out. I've found that other children who really want to participate in the spirit of the Way often find themselves forced to go along with a disruptive friend.

At Station Thirteen, remove the travelers' crosses and send them to the "tomb," which may be a living-room floor. End by telling of the apostles' fear during the time that Jesus was in the tomb and of their great joy when he arose from the dead.

This is called role playing, a relatively new teaching tool. Adapt it to your family or parish, and I hope you have a truly Good Friday.

On Easter Bread, Grass, and Birds

Five years ago when family religious ed was still in the "We've never done it that way before" stage, I talked in Atlanta on traditions and customs. Afterwards, a delightful nun, about 70 years old, and with a distinct accent, came running up the aisle.

She grasped my hands and as she pumped them up and down said, "I'm so glad you're telling these American mommas and poppas to do these things. I left Italy as a child. Yet my dearest memories are of making Easter bread, growing Easter grass, and catching Easter birds."

I pass them along to you in hopes your family can find the time to initiate an Easter custom or two.

Easter Grass "Our little church was too poor to buy lilies," explained Sister, "so during Lent each child grew a little cardboard box of grass. If you plant grass seed and grow it in the dark, it grows tall and white. On Easter Sunday we each carried our box—oh, so proudly, hoping ours would be the tallest or the whitest—and put it on the altar. Soon the whole altar was banked in white, but every child knew just exactly where his or her box sat."

Can we adapt this simple custom? A parish in St. Paul places empty flower vases on the altars at Easter and invites each family to come up together and fill them with flowers. If your parish doesn't do this sort of thing, how about growing some Easter grass for your own family centerpiece?

Easter Bread   "We had two tasks we loved on Holy Saturday," continued Sister. "We caught the Easter bird and baked the Easter bread. We baked a sweet yeast bread with a whole egg in it, shell and all. We decorated the top with sugar, raisins, and nuts. Sometimes we shaped it to look like a tomb or a church. We ate the bread on Easter after Mass and were always so excited when we found the egg safely baked inside."

Families can adapt this one easily. If kneading bread isn't your thing (as it isn't mine), you can buy the frozen dough, let it thaw, and give each member a hand in decorating your family's Easter bread.

Easter Birds   "On Good Friday and Holy Saturday, the family went out to the woods to catch a sparrow. We made homemade traps, and if we caught more than one we gave them to families without a bird." Here she actually shivered. "Oh, it was glorious . . . all those birds singing and flying straight up to heaven."

I think this one defies adaptation, but it certainly adds to the joyful memories of a child's Eastertime, and parents might consider hatching some fertile eggs in a homemade incubator. Simply line a cardboard carton with asbestos ceiling tile, cut a hole in the cover, and drop in a lightbulb to keep the temperature at whatever degree the hatchery people suggest. Then count down from twenty-one days, the amount of time it takes eggs to hatch.

Carefully turn the eggs once a day, but don't make the mistake we did one year. We kept the cover off to watch the eggs hatch, and several chickens died before they hatched. A piece of glass on top prevents this.

And have many a joyous Easter with your grass, bread, and chickens.

Let's Have a St. Patrick's Party

Forgive me if I seem ethnic, but St. Patrick is too valuable to die in the Hallmark stores. He's an endangered species, sitting where Christmas sat several decades ago before it became secularized.

Let's not forget that there once was a St. Valentine and he, too, had a day in his honor. Today we define him as candy, hearts, and parties. Let's not let our young grow up remembering St. Patrick as green beer and shamrocks.

I don't mean we should turn St. Pat's Day into a grim observance, heaven forbid! Rather, let's use it as an occasion for family fun and a little Catholic heritage to boot. Let's plan a family or multi-family party.

First, some background on this saint. There are dozens of legends surrounding the man. I'm using the account from an excellent new paperback, *Saint of the Day*, edited by Leonard Foley, O.F.M. (St. Anthony Messenger Press, $1.95).

St. Patrick's life was full of drama, enough to satisfy the most televisioned child. Alas, I hate to admit that he wasn't Irish at all. He was born in England or Scotland, probably around 389, and died around 461. Here's a capsule from Father Foley's book:

> At sixteen, he and a large number of his father's slaves and vassals were captured by Irish raiders and sold as slaves in Ireland. Forced to work as a shepherd, he suffered greatly from hunger and cold.
>
> After six years, Patrick escaped, probably to France and later returned to Britain at the age of 22. His captivity had meant spiritual conversion. . . . (He) was consecrated bishop at the age of 43. His great desire was to proclaim the Good News to the Irish.
>
> He suffered much opposition from pagan druids. . . . He was a man of action, with little inclination toward learning. . . . There is hope, rather than irony, in the fact that his burial place is said to be in strife-torn Ulster, in County Down.

For your party, put together some of the following:

His story   No brief account here does justice to Patrick's life. Try to get the book, *Saint of the Day*, mentioned above, or any of the new books coming out on the saints' lives.

Symbols   Some of the symbols you can use are: the shamrock, signifying the Holy Trinity; the mitre, because Patrick was a bishop; the lamb, also signifying bishop because of Christ's injunction, "Feed my lambs"; and the fire, a reminder that Patrick lit a fire on the mountaintop in defiance of the pagan druids whom he eventually converted.

Activities   Make shamrock-shaped sandwiches, using a cookie cutter. (Even the youngest can help with these.) Or make a lamb cake or an Irish stew if it's to be a multi-family celebration. Centerpieces and place mats with symbols and events of Patrick's life can be done by one person or by one family.

If four or five families are getting together, put one family in charge of music and have a singalong. Blessing shamrocks is a lovely old Irish custom, one your family will love. Each can bless his or her own, or a parent can bless the pile, mentioning how St. Pat used the shamrock to teach the mystery of the Trinity.

Cards, bingo, singing, and dancing are good family party activities. And it wouldn't hurt to say a few prayers for modern-day Ireland.

The traditional prayer is the one from the "Breastplate of St. Patrick":

Christ shield me this day: Christ with me, Christ before me, Christ behind me, Christ in me, Christ beneath me, Christ above me, Christ on my right, Christ on my left, Christ when I lie down, Christ when I arise, Christ in the heart of every person who thinks of me, Christ in the mouth of every person who speaks of me, Christ in the eye that sees me, Christ in the ear that hears me.

'Tis the Month of Our Mother

Let's use May to reintroduce Mary to our families. We keep waiting for the "Church" to do it or for those mysterious *Theys* who seem to abound more in conversation than in reality: "When are *They* going to get back to the rosary?" and "Why don't *They* have novenas any more?"

Meanwhile, *They* are wondering about us. "Why don't *They* teach their children the Hail Mary?" and "Why did *They* stop saying the rosary?"

Why indeed? Somewhere in the Church crunch of the past decade Mary got lost. She moved from being a personal mother to being someone else's mother.

Thousands of children are growing up without even knowing her. Yet these children's parents invoke her automatically when the fever goes over 101, when the teenager is out on icy roads, and when their own lives are in need of sustenance.

I don't see why we have to choose between old and new ways of honoring Mary. Why not have a blend of both? Here is a list of activities for renewing a friendship with Mary in our families and parish. Why not give the list some family consideration?

- Dig out the old black missal and pray the Litany to our Blessed Mother.
- Make up a new litany using today's experiences and terminology. (One child thought "Tower of Ivory" meant soap.) "Mother of the Media, pray for us" makes a lot of sense.
- For grace, say the beautiful and ageless Memorare: "Remember, O most gracious Virgin Mary, that never was it known that anyone who fled to your protection, implored your help, or sought your intercession, was left unaided. Inspired by this confidence, we fly unto you, O Virgin of virgins, our Mother! To you we come, before you we stand, sinful and sorrowful. O Mother of the Word incarnate, despise not our petitions, but in your mercy hear and answer us. Amen."

- Have a neighborhood May crowning, maybe after a neighborhood Mass.
- Read aloud a chapter from Marjorie Holme's love tale, *Two From Galilee*, every week until it's finished.
- Have a family reunion and invite Mary. Sing some of the old hymns, set up a picnic table shrine, and read some Scripture.
- Hold a weekly Mary liturgy with homemade prayers, centerpieces, and some songs.
- Teach your children the old hymns: "On This Day, O Beautiful Mother," "Ave Maria," and "Mother, Dear, O Pray for Me."
- Have your children teach you the new hymn, "Let It Be."
- Try the family rosary one more time.
- Offer to set up a small group or parish novena to Mary sometime this month.
- Make a family banner to Mary.
- Consider a parish day of recollection and reconciliation with the mother of God.
- Fashion individual shoebox tableaux of scenes from Mary's life. Display them around the home.
- Set up a little Mary shrine in the room of someone in a nursing home and bring fresh flowers and conversation every week.
- Say a daily petition to Mary for a special family intention.
- Read the Arch and Purple Puzzle Tree Bible books that pertain to Mary.
- Tell the children about the effect Mary has had on your life.
- Get hold of *My Nameday, Come for Dessert* by Helen McLoughlin (The Liturgical Press, Collegeville, Minnesota) and celebrate some of the twenty-eight different feastdays dedicated to Mary: Our Lady of Carmel, Our Lady of Guadalupe, and others.
- Build a backyard shrine to Mary.

CHAPTER 8

The Art of Reconciliation

We parents are no strangers to the reconciliation process. Probably the family, more than any other institution, experiences the little wearing and tearing ruptures that keep life from being the warm pleasant utopia we'd like it to be.

One rupture that affects the family is the division between family members. Translated in the kitchen, this means family fighting: child against child, parent against parent, and child against parent.

I can't think of anything so damaging to our hopes of harmonious family life as constant quarreling, punishment, and retaliation. We don't usually see family fighting as a religious theme, but within the framework of the family we can see quite clearly the consequences of sin and the process of reconciliation.

Suppose a child deliberately offends another or breaks a rule (Commandment). This causes a rupture (sin) in the family (Christian community). This rupture (sin) causes a weakening in the bond between child and parent or child and child (between us and God). The child suffers from isolation from the family (our separation from God). When the child takes the steps to be reconciled with the family, the relationship is restored. This reconciliation usually demands sorrow from the child (contrition and penance) and forgiveness from the parent or injured child (absolution). So it is that our sins demand sorrow from us and forgiveness from our heavenly Father.

We can use this analogy to point out to our families the great gift of God's forgiveness. Children love parents, but they stand in loving awe of forgiving adults. That's one reason they find grandparents, who tend to be more forgiving than parents, so loveable.

In the past we learned about Penance chiefly in terms of the future consequences of sin—punishment after death in purgatory or hell. It wasn't stressed that the painful isolation we felt from God was part of the cost of our sin and that the Sacrament of Reconciliation ended that isolation and brought us together again. It is this aspect of Penance that we can emphasize with our children.

When they slam into their rooms, cutting themselves off from our love, we can wait for them to return and effect reconciliation. Later we can talk with them about the pain of such a separation and have them express their feelings of love and relief when it ended.

"When was one time you really felt lonely—all alone with nobody to love you?" a parent can ask.

"That time I broke the window and was scared and ran away and hid," replies the child.

"What made you come home?"

"I needed to. I was lonely and I was hungry."

The parent nods. "I know what you mean. That's the way I feel when I do something wrong, commit some sin. First I'm scared and then I'm sorry, and then I need to come back to God and tell him so."

"You mean big people feel that way, too?"

"Lots of times. That's why I go to the Sacrament of Penance, you know."

"When I get big will I be able to go, too?"

This approach differs from the old one—"Now that you're seven you have to go to Confession"—by making the Sacrament a positive experience for the child to anticipate, not a routine one to fear.

Last summer at an ecumenical religious camp for girls I conducted a seminar on family relationships. In preparation , I asked each girl to finish this statement: "If I could change one thing about my family, it would be . . . ."

Counselors collected the unsigned statements and gave them to me a week before my session. There were the usual "that I wouldn't have to do the dishes" and "that we had lots of money" answers, but the overwhelming number concerned family fighting. To share a few:

"That my brothers would stop hitting me."

"That my mom and I wouldn't fight so much."

"That us kids wouldn't say such mean things to each other."

"That my mom and dad wouldn't fight."

As a parent, I didn't realize family fighting affected children so much. (I know it affects me.) Because we're the ones that always seem to be stopping the battles, we tend to think kids enjoy them.

Closer scrutiny of the replies revealed an interesting difference in blame among the three age groups: third through fifth grade, sixth through eighth grade, and high schoolers.

The younger girls tended to blame the other person. "I wish my brother would stop hitting me," or "that my mother would quit yelling," or "that my sister wouldn't be so bossy." This is in keeping with the age group that sees a simple cause and effect: "He's mean and I'm persecuted."

Parents are familiar with the child's tendency to attribute a parent's anger to the child's last action, such as noisy chewing. It doesn't occur to the child that he or she's been piling up irritations all day and that the chewing simply is a last straw. The action immediately prior to the scolding is the bad one, in the child's mind.

The sixth-through-eighth-grade children mentioned family fighting but tended to implicate themselves. Again, to share: "that I was easier to get along with" or "that I wouldn't fight with my mother so much."

This is also predictable. The preadolescent, who is at an introspective age, finds himself or herself unloveable and figures everyone else must, too. This age can drive parents up the wall, but it does show growth in the reconciliation process. The girls have gone from blaming others to sharing in the blame for family ruptures.

Finally, the teenagers tended to be more objective. They didn't point the finger at one person or the other but named the fighting itself the culprit. "If I could change one thing about my family, it would be the constant fighting that divides us... " was typical of the high schoolers' answers.

Parents are familiar with the tendency at this age to blame the inanimate: "The clock was slow," or "The car broke down." It, too, can be trying, but again it shows growth in reconciliation. It says, "Let's not blame one another, but let's look at the fighting and see how it can be prevented."

This is real growth in the reconciliation process, one that parents can recognize and foster. It says, "Let's watch for those words, those inferences, and those situations that lead up to the fighting and try to stop them."

Once we as parents realize that children don't really like fighting in the home and that each age group fights on a different level *but* that we all have to live together, we may be better able to recognize and offset potential ruptures.

Here are some suggestions for a lesson on *Family Fighting and Reconciliation*.

Set aside some time, at least thirty minutes for each child. If you have children close together in age, teach them together, or teach the whole family together, including parents. Sometimes I like to have an intimate one-to-one class with my children. At other times, more are better.

A good way to start is to check out from any library Charlotte Zolotow's simple children's book, *The Quarreling Book*. (Or get your parish to buy copies.) This little story shows how bad moods begin and how they are passed from person to person until they bump into someone who returns happiness for gloom. This breaks the chain and reverses the procedure. A reconciliation takes place, and the story ends with the sun coming out.

If this story isn't available, find a substitute (like Maurice Sendak's *Where the Wild Things Are*) or tell the children a story about a time you woke up in a bad mood and how it affected your day and the day of those around you. They'll listen in awe as Parent admits weakness.

After the story, use this exercise, orally or in writing, depending upon the age, ability, and openness of the child.

Reconciliation-and-Me Survey

- What time of day am I crossest? (Morning, after school, etc.)
- Why am I cross then? (Hungry, tired, tired of being around people?)
- What time of week am I crossest?
- What time of year am I crossest?
- What words from Mom make me mad? ("In a minute," or "I've told you a thousand times.")
- From Dad? From sister, brother, teacher, piano teacher, friend?
- What words of mine make Mom mad? ("I can't find my . . . ," "Do we hafta go to Church?")
- Taking the above words or phrases, how would you like Mom to answer instead of with those words? How could you answer Mom with better words than those that irritate her?
- What's the best time of day, week, and year for you to stay away from others?
- What special words or names do you use with each member of the family when you want to please them?

The above is a good exercise for the whole family to do together. Have each person complete it and read it aloud as part of a family reconciliation liturgy. If your family isn't ready for that yet, try it between one parent and a child.

The object is to show one another the abrasiveness of words and to recognize that we all are abrasive, more so at one time than another. Awareness is the first step to reconciliation.

Follow up the above with one of these:

Art theme Draw a line down the center of the paper. On the left have your child draw your family as it looks when it's unhappy; on the right when it's happy. (Brace yourself for this one, parents. Mom and Dad can come out looking like monsters while the angels tread about.)

Homemade prayers "Dear God, help me not to be so cross after school when I'm tired of people. Don't let me get so mad when my sister calls me Dummy, and help me not to call her Fatty back.... "

Role playing Have child take parent's part and parent take child's and reenact these family scenes: spilled milk, stalling bedtime, homework hassle, getting ready for church, and any others you can dream up.

Some basic hints on preparing for a family liturgy: Let each member have a responsibility, e.g. candles, songs, place mats with symbols, centerpiece, readings, prayers. Even the youngest can blow out the candles and feel a part of the whole experience.

Schedule it for some relaxed time in the family week. Nothing will ruin it faster than a parent saying through clenched teeth, "I don't care what TV show is on, we're going to get this celebration over with." Some families find the fifteen minutes before bedtime best. Others like the period right after dinner, while still others find Sunday afternoon a good time for a family liturgy.

Use a home catechism lesson to get ready. The assignment of each child can be his or her part in the liturgy. Have an older child check biblical readings on forgiveness and choose one or two such as The Prodigal Son (Luke 15:11-32) and the Beatitudes (Matthew 5:1-12). The same child will be responsible for choosing the readers and seeing that they have marked copies for practice.

This is a good time to check your family Bible assortment. Do you have one that children can read easily? I like any one of these four: the inexpensive *Children's Bible* (Liturgical Press); the *Golden Children's Bible*, easily found at supermarkets; *The Taizé Picture Bible* (Herder and Herder), and *Bible Stories, Retold by David Kossoff* (Follett Publishing Company).

For junior high on up, the paperback *Good News for Modern Man* is popular. Ask your DRE to buy samples of children's bibles so you can look them over before buying.

Next there's music. Ask one child to choose an opening, a middle, and an ending song and write out the words for each member of the family. Some children love to do this, individualizing the sheets and embellishing them with symbols. The child might choose for a reconciliation theme "Shalom," "They'll Know We Are Christians," and the "Our Father."

If you are short on song material, ask your DRE or pastor for past issues of the *Missalette*. There is a variety of songs in the back, or again, ask your parish to buy a few songbooks for parents to check out, use, and return. (Remember when you wondered *what* the DREs would be doing if you were teaching your children? They're going to be running to keep ahead of your needs.)

Next there's art. Have one child responsible for a centerpiece on reconciliation. Some families also have a large sheet of paper and felt pen or crayon in front of each member for some kind of drawing project during the liturgy. Remember, we parents have to get down to the children's level at times, and this is a good time to do so.

Finally, there are the parents who put it all together. It can go like this:

Open ceremony:	Lighting of candles
Opening hymn:	"Shalom"
Biblical reading:	Prodigal Son
Art time:	Drawing one scene from Prodigal Son; explaining and sharing drawings
Hymn:	"They'll Know We Are Christians by Our Love"
Homemade prayers:	Written during family catechism lessons, or spoken spontaneously
Parent:	Short talk on What Family Reconciliation Means to Me
Final hymn:	Dim lights, join hands, and sing "Our Father"
End ceremony:	Extinguish candles

CHAPTER 9

The Sunday Mass Hassle

The number-one question parents ask in family or teenage religion sessions is an anguished "What do you do when they don't want to go to Mass?"

It's an encouraging sign that they will even ask it. Once upon a time they were too ashamed to expose their "failure" as good Catholic parents to admit it openly. There's no tidy answer. If there were, the question wouldn't persist.

The self-defeating "Force the child to go" and "Let the child decide" aren't the only choices. Let's take a hard look at three aspects of it: Why do teenagers fight Mass? Why do parents react as they do? How can we make Mass more significant to youngsters?

Why do teenagers fight Mass? Frequently they use it as a weapon, knowing that it bothers Mom and Dad. The more religion means to the parents, the more powerful the weapon, and the clever child knows how to maintain a constant tension level by questioning its value.

Other offspring question it honestly. They wonder why they have to go if it doesn't mean much to them. In reality, they're asking parents, "Why do you go to Mass?" If parents retort angrily, "Because I say so!" or feebly, "Because the Church says so," the children's suspicions are justified—that their parents don't get much out of Mass either.

So parents should be ready with an honest reply to the inevitable "Why do I have to go to Mass?" That reply should tell the child why the parents feel Mass is valuable to them.

"I go to Mass because I need it. Without it, I wouldn't take the time to worship God. And I really believe in God. So if I believe in him, I have to worship him" could be an honest non-theological reply of parents. The youth will have to accept their parents' sincerity, and that's often what they're questioning when they fight Mass.

Once children accept their parents' reasons, they're apt to follow through with "Okay, but why me? I don't believe you need to worship together in a church to love God."

Here parents must be very careful. Instead of treating the question with the emotion reserved for religion, they can treat it as if the child said he or she wasn't getting anything out of school and wanted to quit.

When that situation arises, the parents don't feel personally threatened and guilty. They explain that despite the child's boredom, he or she will one day see the need for math and spelling. Until children discover that value, it's the parents' job to see that they're there, experiencing and learning.

This kind of response tells the children: 1) that the parents see value in going to Mass; 2) that parents don't expect them to see the same value until they mature (that kills them); and 3) until then, it's the parents' job to help them grow into spiritual maturity.

As a clincher, the parents can add, "When you were young, you didn't see any value in shots, dentists, or multiplication tables, but it was our job to see that you had them. Now you don't see any value in Mass, and it's our job to see that you have it. Maybe it won't come to mean anything to you, but maybe it will. And we're not going to deny you that future."

Isn't that a better response than "Because I say so!"?

Now let's examine why parents react so strongly to a child's "Why do I have to go to Mass?" or "I hate church." This strong reaction is often emotional, even in the most thoughtful parents, and they hear themselves say in angry retort, "I don't care if you hate it, you're going because I say so."

And the satisfied child smiles to himself or herself, "Aha, I got to Dad this time." Or they go off to Mass in the flesh only. Their exaggerated boredom tells the congregation clearly that they're there only under the duress of cruel and oppressive parents.

If parents react rationally and unemotionally, as they do when a child tells them that he or she doesn't want to go to the dentist ("Get your coat"), the child doesn't win the psychological battle. It's an axiom that the more emotionally involved the parents are on an issue, the more successful the child is in exploiting it.

Why do we parents get so emotional when our children question religion, be it CCD, Mass, or the blessing of throats? Partly because we feel guilty. We have accepted the unacceptable—a responsibility for another's lifelong faith.

Nobody can take that responsibility—not priest, pope, or parent. All we can do is nurture the best religious environment possible and pray. The rest is up to God. The child has to take the responsibility for faith upon himself or herself eventually. Once he or she's independent, the parents' influence has faded, if not vanished.

We parents tend to see the fight against Mass as evidence that the child has rejected our faith and consequently our guidance. So we take it very personally. We're hurt.

Our pride suffers when our friends no longer see our children at Mass. Our pride pinches when the pastor remarks on the dwindling family, and it stabs when Grandma asks what Mass Johnny attends.

We parents also see Mass as *the* sign of Catholic identity, central to our faith, and we want to pass this treasure along to our children. From our childhood Church history days, we recall stories of the risks earlier Christians took just to go to Mass. When we see our own children spurn it, we're saddened. Mass is more important to us than any other single religious activity.

The irony is that Mass is almost the only visible sign left that one is a Catholic. Once upon a Church, the Catholic attended not only Sunday Mass, but parochial school, novenas, bazaars, Forty Hours, Confession, and dozens of other functions which labeled him or her Catholic. All that's really left to distinguish between an "in" and an "out" Catholic is Mass attendance.

If, as parents, we've let all the rest go in our family religious life only to become upset when our child stops going to Mass, we're really not that interested in his or her personal faith. We're more interested in our own consciences and pride. Underneath it all, we know we haven't done that much to foster a deep experience of faith in the home, so we demand that the Church furnish it during one hour a week. And when the child stops attending Mass, we blame the Church.

Finally, we get emotional because we don't get that turned on by Mass ourselves. For years, as they were growing up, our children heard us criticize the Mass, sensed our boredom, and listened to us talk of it as an obligation rather than as an opportunity. Now when we're trying to stress to them our regard for the Mass, they have an understandable suspicion of our motives.

But there is hope on the altar horizon. Youth are trickling back to Mass—not every youth, not every week, but enough to make their presence noticeable.

How can parents take positive action (not more force) in making Mass more significant to today's children?

I've long felt that Catholic parents are ignoring their best source of help in the Church—other Catholic parents—, and I would like to encourage the parish to offer a one-shot session led by parents on the perplexing question, "What do we do when they don't want to go to Mass?"

I've found that parents tend to steer away from theological meanderings and go right to the heart of the problem—how do we get children to like Mass? Here are some suggestions I've gleaned from parents.

A key word is *involvement*. The more a family or a child becomes involved in the liturgy itself, the more willing they are to attend. If a child is part of the music group, if Dad is a lector, if the family brings up the gifts, or even if the child is asked to tidy up after Mass, it's an act of involvement. Otherwise it's something to watch.

It's astonishing that we overlook this in our liturgies. In education we know that if we take a turned-off child and give him or her a role in class, be it as movie operator or eraser cleaner, we spark an interest in the class. So we must create opportunities for involvement.

There are ways a parish can do this: by giving many different people an opportunity to lead the music; by encouraging families to make banners; by asking various families to pick up *Missalettes*; by inviting children as well as adults to act as lectors; by inviting families to submit special prayers to be read during Mass—in short, by making Mass the family's own.

In many parishes we find the same parishioners bringing up the gifts and passing the basket week after week; understandably, we soon come to believe that the Mass is theirs and that we're there to watch them.

Secondly, there's the question of *variety*. Many children who are turned off have been going to the same Mass over and over for so many years that they can just about pinpoint when the celebrant's going to cough.

Sure, it may mean more driving, but what we do for football games we can surely do for Mass. If you live in a metropolitan area (or even in a rural area), you have an opportunity to expose your children to many styles of churches, preaching, and congregations. They don't have to grow up thinking there's only one kind of Catholic parish, pastor, or liturgy.

And let the children know that you are deliberately giving them a wider experience of worship within their own Church.

A third idea is family *enjoyment*. Parents with the most turned-on children tell me it's because Sunday morning is used as relaxed family time for activity built around the Mass. They go out for breakfast occasionally, go to the park with sandwiches in summer, visit friends and museums in the winter, and just generally give their families some uninterrupted time together this one morning a week.

Finally, there's the *home Mass*. Give your family the experience of a small intimate family liturgy once a year and it will help them feel what Mass can really be. It's difficult to get kids excited about the large impersonal Sunday liturgy when they can't even see it.

The job of enriching the Mass is largely up to us, the parents, not Father, and it is only as important to us as the amount of time we're willing to put into it.

CHAPTER 10

"Because I Said So—I Think" Helping Your Family to Grow Morally

Parents have a way of saying things that years later they wish they'd never said. I'm no exception. I recall, with embarrassment, an incident that took place at Grandma's home when our daughter was young.

It seems that Beth, then three or so, was being selfish with her toys, refusing to share them with visiting cousins. I reasoned with her, pleaded with her, and finally insisted, much to Grandma's dismay, that she either share or go to her room. Feeling defensive, I told my mother righteously, "But I'm not being too strict with her. She's been told over and over that it's wrong not to share, so she *knows* it's wrong."

I hope my mother has forgotten that statement. I realize now that Beth knew nothing of the sort. She knew I thought it was wrong, but she herself didn't accept it as wrong. How could I be right and she wrong when she ended up losing her toys to others?

She gave them up, of course, but only because I forced it. Beth was at a stage of moral development typical of her age. Reward and punishment determine young children's moral thinking in their early years. And children perceive reward and punishment only in very concrete, tangible ways—a toy in the hand, a stern voice from a towering adult. So Beth obeyed.

Years later Beth would be in a higher stage. She would give up her "toys"—her loud music, noisy gum, or whatever—to win peer, parent, or teacher approval. Her moral thinking would progress beyond reward and punishment, beyond the bargaining and backscratching stage, to the morality of the group, to the meeting of the expectations of people important to her. She would be a "good girl" to please her teachers and us, and a "good friend" to please her peers.

I wish we had known more about the stages in moral development when our children were younger. It would have helped both us and them: us because we would have better understood their reasoning, and them because we would have been able to interact with their thinking more realistically. I find a basic understanding of moral growth valuable in understanding my children's behaviors today. I realize they're behaving normally when they exhibit certain behaviors that I don't consider moral, such as cheating. I've also learned that if, rather than condemning the cheating itself or assigning a motive to it, I reach them from a higher level of reasoning, I'll help lead them into a higher level of morality.

Much has been written about moral growth in the past five or ten years, but I find widespread confusion about it among parents, the very ones who can benefit most from it. They aren't sure just what moral growth is, and many feel it's too complicated for them to understand. It does require some thinking, but no more than the other developmental processes. If we can read up on and prepare ourselves for physical development (standing, crawling, walking), social development (the thirteen-month-old's suspicion of anyone but Mom, for example), and verbal development (sounds, words, thoughts), we have the tools for preparing ourselves to anticipate and deal with moral development.

Reading, discussing, observing, and evaluating are the methods by which we've learned many parental skills. If parents read this chapter and find it worthwhile to use in their own family, they can seek additional articles and books on the subject, ask for a lecture or course through their parish, begin to observe what they learn at home among their children, and evaluate their own effectiveness as moral guides.

First, what is moral development? Simply put, *moral development is the process people go through in developing a conscience, a sense of what is right, what is wrong, and why.* Why do some children and adults believe it's morally okay to steal, for instance, while others think it's wrong? Why do some children make better moral decisions than their older brothers and sisters?

The formation of a conscience is a developmental process in which people move from one stage to another. As with physical growth, some children grow faster than others. And people can stop growing morally and become permanently fixed at a certain stage. That's why we find some grownup criminals with a less-developed sense of right and wrong than many eight-year-olds have. Somewhere along the line their moral development stopped.

Religious educators and many parents have long suspected that there are identifiable stages of a person's moral development. But only in the past decade have these stages, studied by psychologist Lawrence Kohlberg and theologian James Fowler, become understandable on the lay level. Both men based their research on the work of Swiss educator Dr. Jean Piaget, who gave us the stages of a child's cognitive or reasoning ability.

Lawrence Kohlberg theorized that humans advance through stages of moral development. Subsequent testing and research have given increasing weight to his theories.

He describes six stages, which I give below. Don't be put off by the strange labels. Directly after each, I give an example of how a person reasons at that stage. We can't put an age on any particular stage. Naturally, a child will begin at Stage One, and people do not regress to stages they have outgrown. These are about the only absolutes in the developmental process. Some grownups will remain at Stage One, while many young people will progress to Stage Four by high-school graduation. It's fair to say that most children are likely to land in the first two or three stages.

Stages of Morality According to Lawrence Kohlberg

Stage One: **Punishment-and-obedience orientation**
People at this stage feel dominated by those
stronger or in authority. "It's wrong because
I'll get spanked if I do it," or "Mom will get
mad at me." This is a stage typical of
preschoolers.

Stage Two: **Self-satisfaction orientation** This is the
"What's in it for me?" stage. People at this
stage recognize that others have needs and
feelings, but they try to use these to their
own benefit. "If I do what my folks say,
they'll be nice to me." "I'll share my toys
with you, if you'll play with me." This stage
often begins in the early school years.

Stage Three: **Group-expectations orientation** This is the
"good boy/good girl" stage. People conform
to group standards because they value the
group's opinion. Reasoning based on others'
expectations can cause conflicts when a
person belongs to different groups with
different values. "I want my friends to
approve of what I do." "I'll do it because it
pleases those important to me."
"Everybody's doing it." Stage Three
reasoning is found among many adolescents.
Many adults remain at Stage Three, basing
their moral reasoning on others' approval.

Stage Four: **Law-and-authority orientation** People see
the value of law for preserving the common
good in society and for protecting their best
selves. This is a positive stage in which
people internalize values and principles.
"Because it's the law." "School rules."
"Duty." "Company policy." This is the
highest stage most adults reach.

Stage Five: **Social-contract orientation** People see that
individual laws are not absolute. Society can

	agree to change laws to bring greater justice to a greater number of people. Laws and obligations are made through free agreement and contract. "It's the law, but I'm trying to change it because it's unfair." People at Stage Five are affected by the injustice of others close to them rather than by more universal problems.
Stage Six:	**Universal-principles orientation** People see that ethical principles apply to everyone equally and are higher than any individual law. "I'll do it because it's the fair thing for all people." "Justice is justice no matter who you are."

Let's take a rather familiar behavior, lying, and run it through the six stages.

Stage One: "It's wrong to lie because I might get caught and punished."
Stage Two: "It's wrong to lie because I'll feel guilty and that'll be unpleasant."
Stage Three: "It's wrong to lie because my friends don't lie, and I don't want them to think less of me." (Or, as is often the case in adolescent peer-group shifting, "It's right to lie because my friends do, and I don't want them to think less of me.")
Stage Four: "It's wrong to lie because if everyone lied, our family and society's life would be in disorder. To operate smoothly, we have to believe each other."
Stage Five: "It's wrong to lie unless lying serves the greater good of most people."
Stage Six: "It's wrong to lie because telling the truth is a way of respecting oneself and the rights and dignity of other human persons."

Before elaborating on the stages, let me stress what they're *not*. They're *not* a new religion, but simply a tool for understanding the level of moral reasoning. They're *not* accurate for categorizing individuals. (We don't want to set up religion class for Stage Ones, Stage Twos, for example.) And they're *not* absolute. One might think on one level and behave on a lower level, as is the case of a person who has lofty ideals regarding racial tolerance but switches the children to private schools when busing hits personally.

By knowing these stages, the parent can lead a child from one stage to the next rather than attack the child for behaving on a certain level. We know that the toddler will go through Stage One morality: "That's a no-no. Don't touch or I'll spank your hands." We accept this, but we don't want to be spanking hands at eleven: we expect the eleven-year-old to be operating on a higher level. We need to realize that children can't jump from the no-no stage to principled action without passing through other stages. That's like expecting them to jump directly from their first word to complete sentences.

Most children will follow the no-no stage with an even-more-frustrating stage of hedonism, Stage Two: "What satisfies my needs is okay." On a child's level this can result in good or bad actions. Children may stop lying, not because they see wrong in it, but because the greater freedom their parents will allow as a result will be self-satisfying. On an adult level, it's likely to be the "What's in it for me?" mentality.

It's futile to deal with the immaturity of this level. Better to lead the child into Stage Three: "It's right if it pleases those I like." If children stop lying because they know it disappoints the important persons in their lives or stop tattling because their friends don't like it, they're into Stage Three behavior. This is common adolescent behavior, where the peer group takes great precedence.

Many people never get beyond Stage Three. Their morality is based upon the reaction of people they consider important. Others never get beyond Stages One or Two. One study even indicates that most adult convicts and many adult prison personnel remain fixed in Stage One, the obey-or-get-punished stage, or Stage Two, the let's-make-a-deal stage.

One rule given us by Kohlberg is that levels of morality should not be used to categorize but to help lead persons into ever-higher stages *by responding to them at the stage immediately above their present stage.* I like to compare it to helping pokey children upstairs. We have the option of either criticizing them for being where they are or reaching out from a step above and helping them move up.

If they're operating on Stage One, "I didn't cheat because I was afraid I'd get caught and punished," we can respond from a Stage-Two perspective: "If you cheated, it might make you feel guilty, and that isn't a very pleasant feeling, is it?"

If they're operating on a Stage-Four level, "What can I do? It's school rules," we can respond with "Sometimes we have to question the rules and change them, even though it may be unpleasant for us."

Now, let's apply moral growth not to the child but to ourselves and our own basic moral behavior. Why don't I shoplift? Why don't I cheat on my income tax? Why do I discriminate? All these involve levels of morality. Let's put Kohlberg's stages into the context of why we behave morally.

Stage One, Punishment and obedience: "If I don't, I'll go to hell. If I do, I'll go to heaven."
Stage Two, Self-satisfaction: "I'll behave morally because I'm more likely to get ahead at home, on the job, or in the community."
Stage Three, Group expectations: "I'll behave morally because my Church, my family, and my friends value moral behavior."
Stage Four, Law and authority: "I'll behave morally because it's Church law, and every religion needs its set of laws and doctrines."
Stage Five, Social contract: "Just following Church laws isn't enough. I must work to keep them viable for me and others."
Stage Six, Ethical principles: "I'll behave morally because it will best serve God and humankind."

We can take any behavior and run it through the stages to find out where we operate personally and to trace our personal moral growth. Take lying again. When did I stop lying because I was afraid of going to hell for it? When because it displeased parents and friends? Where am I now? Have I stopped there for life, or can I go on to a higher level?

Again, most of us settle on Stage Four, Church law. That's why our faith is so shaken when the law changes (Communion in the hand) or disappears (fasting). Once the law of fasting was lifted, was the morality of it also lifted? Were we permanently fixed on Stage Four? It's interesting to note that few of us fast today. Yet we once believed fasting was a highly moral act.

The Stage-Six person is the rare being who is so principled and loving that he or she doesn't need to consider his or her actions. Stage-Six people always do what is best for their neighbor. They would continue fasting, perhaps, because it helps them focus on human needs or it allows their neighbor more food.

The Stage-Five person has to take the large and frightening step from externally-imposed rules to internally-Christian behavior, from laws to love. We're involved in our own moral growth. It isn't someone else's responsibility to help us move into a higher stage of morality. It requires a lot of reflecting, prayer, and acting.

Parents who invest the time to better understand moral growth will be gratified at the results within themselves and their families. They'll feel more in control of their own and of their children's sense of right and wrong. When our larger culture shifts moral approval from one action to another with alarming frequency, our children must look to their closest moral guides for help. The closest moral guides are their parents. Are we ready to meet our children's needs?

CHAPTER 11

"Go Get My Wallet"

We're halfway between the casserole and the cantaloupe when the doorbell rings. The child closest to the door jumps up to answer it. "Hey, Dad, it's the cancer envelope." "Go get my wallet," calls Dad. A dollar later, we've done our family thing for cancer. And the children watch and learn.

Starving children stare out of the TV screen at us as we sit nestled in beanbag chairs, munching popcorn. Not missing a kernel, a child laughs and comments, "Look at their big tummies."

"Shhhh," we admonish. "Don't you know their tummies are like that because they're starving?"

"Then why doesn't somebody give them some food?"

"Well," we stammer, "we do—through the Church and government."

"No," he insists, "I don't mean that. Why don't *we* give them some food?"

We change the subject. And the children watch and learn.

Each year thousands of children around the country walk or bike for the poor. They start at 6 a.m., often walking until 6 p.m. If they make it to the end, their feet are blistered, but their spirits are high. They have done something for the needy. But... only three-fourths of them get around to collecting the funds pledged per mile by neighbors and friends.

"If you can walk twenty-five miles, why can't you walk around the block and collect?" ask bewildered parents.

"Oh, that part's no fun," respond the kids.

Walking for the sake of the walk is one thing. Walking for the sake of the poor is quite another.

Christian parents in America live with an uncomfortable dichotomy between affluent living and Christian beliefs. We want to rear children to be generous, thoughtful, and responsive to the needs of others, but not if it means disrupting our lifestyle and ideology. We want to give them a Christian legacy, but "within reason," a selective Christian legacy. We select which of Christ's messages to emphasize, which to overlook.

We can moralize endlessly about the parable of the Good Samaritan as long as he remains in Scripture. But let some priest or religion text write him into a modern perspective and we're horrified. The Scriptures have been desecrated. Our outrage conveniently cloaks the question, Who is my neighbor?

In working with Catholic parents, I find the question of concern for "my neighbor" far down on the list of parent priorities, an irony when we realize it was the essence of Christ's message and example. I suspect "feeding the poor" would land near the bottom of a typical Catholic parent's list of concerns, outranked by "keeping the schools open," "teaching basics," "getting youth to Mass," and "fighting abortion."

Catholic parents talk about teaching concern for others, but they act on the issues important to them. Thus we find that those parents who are most determined to keep a parish school open are also those most determined to see that diocesan monies don't go elsewhere, like to the elderly or derelict. Others, avowedly anti-abortion, frequently ignore the needs of the already-born.

Why the dichotomy in the Catholic home between statement and action where the needy, the elderly, the handicapped, and the disadvantaged are concerned? We've fallen into a pattern of rationalization. Let's look at my opening examples.

When Buddy gets Dad's wallet and slips a dollar into the cancer envelope, he's exposing some fairly common family attitudes toward giving. The first is that *all giving is lumped together as charity*. Our emphasis centers not on the need or on the spirit but on the act of giving. Dad writes a check for the basket at church, Mom buys Girl Scout raffle tickets, and we put a dollar in the charity envelope. To the children, charity becomes the passing of money from donor to recipient.

Yet much of what we give is not for others but for ourselves. When Dad writes a check for the Sunday Mass collection, he is writing it essentially for himself and his family. It isn't charity; it's Church support. Likewise, when Mom buys raffle tickets from the Girl Scouts or supports the Little League light bulb sale, she isn't showing concern for others as much as supporting neighborhood youth activities. These are money-raising projects for camping trips or new uniforms for the kids on the block, not food and fuel for the people across the tracks or across the ocean.

While the door-to-door envelopes help others, they serve to help us as well. Putting money into a cancer envelope might just save one of our own lives someday.

So not all giving is as charitable as we allow our children to misunderstand. We've fallen into this trap because of the deductible status of contributions, but there's a wide gulf between deductible and charitable monies.

A second attitude is that *need is a seasonal thing*, an attitude unfortunately formed and reinforced by our campaign mentality. By falling into a pattern years ago of campaigning for funds, we've come unintentionally to implant the idea that there is a beginning and an end to need, prescribed by the duration of a particular campaign. We give a good deal of attention to the elderly during Senior Citizens month; but once that's over, it's the migrants' turn, or that of the Viet orphans or the hurricane helpless.

By shutting off the terrible attack on our consciences that the needs of people everywhere mount, we can keep our balance—and our life style. The campaign mentality helps us to do this.

Our own Campaign for Human Development within the Catholic Church is trying to offset this implication by launching a process of bringing issues to the consciousness of the total community and of assisting Christians at all levels to understand the urgent and complex dimensions of poverty and injustice in America. In short, when the Campaign for Human Development ends, poverty doesn't.

A third attitude is widely accepted in many families: *caring and sharing are the parents' responsibility.* The scene with the cancer envelope is typical. Nobody questioned that "getting Dad's wallet" was the right thing to do. If the parents had suggested that each child contribute, they would have been greeted with a chorus of incredulous "You-mean-we-have-to-use-our-own-money?" wails. This reaction is so common that frustrated parents point to it as an example of children's selfishness; but they fail to study its source.

When did generosity become an adults-only thing? When the parents took that role upon themselves. The first time the kindergartner comes home from school excited over a class canned-goods collection, the parent makes a decision and teaches a lesson. If Mother helps the child count his or her money and they buy a can together the next time they shop, she lays a sharing groundwork. If she just buys a can and puts it in the hands of the child on the appointed day, she reinforces the notion that her children's charities are the parents' responsibility.

The cost of this parental behavior is to the children's generous selves. Children know they aren't giving anything up, and they want to. Their image of self as helper is nil. They become recipients, and they know it. Their generosity levels shrink with each succeeding year, and before long they become callous little takers.

A fourth attitude is *giving is fine as long as we have fun doing it.* Those thousands of kids walking together for hunger wouldn't do it alone. The fun is in the group effort. Likewise, when their parents pay $20 for a benefit ball ticket, they're getting an evening out in exchange. Raffle tickets, benefits, bike-a-thons and other functions labeled charitable are rationalized as "Oh well, it's fun; and as long as it's for charity . . . . "

112

The prevalence of this attitude leads heads of organizations into spending more time in trying to find new means to raise money than in helping the needy they're supposed to serve.

Another attitude prevalent in many families: *we have delegated our concern to our Church and government*. This isn't a child's attitude but a parent's. Most children under twelve cannot even understand the idea that an institution can serve as surrogate neighbor's keeper. The idea is too abstract. Therefore, as in the incident of the starving population on television, they ask their parents, "Why don't we feed them?" and the parents tend to become defensive. Parental defensiveness tells the children it is a taboo subject, one to be avoided in the future. Before long, the family stops talking about need, loneliness, hunger, prejudice, and injustice. They become uncomfortable subjects in an otherwise comfortable family.

A final family attitude combines *reliance on the myths about poverty with a distrust of charitable organizations themselves*. This pair of prejudices effectively rationalizes away a family's lack of concern. As long as parents can quote tales about dishonest welfare recipients without looking at the actual facts, they can justify their inaction and lack of caring to their children. Thus they can perpetuate the dichotomy between preaching about being our neighbor's keeper and doing nothing. As long as parents can point the finger of distrust at the March of Dimes, Care, and Catholic Relief Services, mentioning unproven reports of the high salaries of officials in these groups, they don't have to give. They remain honorable in their children's eyes.

If parents are genuinely concerned about their monies going to organizations with an inordinately high expenditure for personnel, they should take steps to check out the organization before giving. A simple call to the organization with a request for their annual report should furnish the information.

Responsible giving requires weighing some needs against others. Giving to a local cause such as migrant needs or flood relief will often replace annual giving to the more traditional groups. Discussing these needs as a family lets everyone share in giving-decisions.

Granted these attitudes, how does the concerned Christian parent replace them with positive attitudes and action for the welfare of others? I suggest:

The Five Commitments.

1. We commit ourselves to making a commitment. It doesn't matter how insignificant it is, we make a commitment to a neighbor, and we keep it. It might only be that this year we as a family will spend two hours visiting a lonely old person in a nursing home or that we will study local pockets of poverty, but it will at least be a commitment.

2. We commit ourselves to raising our family consciousness toward the poor, the disadvantaged, and all those in need. When we put money in the cancer envelope, we talk with our children about cancer—the toll it takes and the hope for its future cure. When we see starving people on television, we don't quickly change the channel. Instead we try, with our children, to imagine the terrible ordeal of parents looking for food for their children in a foodless land; we bring ourselves and our children face to face with the inequity of our overabundance and others' lack of basic necessities.

We stop trying to hide from our children the reality of the poor and helpless elderly, the disabled, the disfigured, the retarded, the disadvantaged Black or Chicano, or the alcoholic. From faceless statistics we make them into real persons, persons we and our children recognize as our neighbors. How can we expect our children to see them as neighbors if they don't see them at all?

3. We commit ourselves to counteracting unchristian attitudes toward others. Because we, as mature adults, are aware that Archie Bunker's prejudices represent a weakness in an essentially good-hearted but very limited man, we find them endearing. We can laugh without malice when he talks about "kikes, hippies, and welfare chiselers." But, of course, his quips are unchristian, belittling, and downright unfair to their victims. It is unfair to our children when we laugh at the program in their presence without making any effort to explain it to them—when, for instance, we don't take time to tell them later that *kike* is a derogatory term we should not apply to Jews, who are merely persons whose beliefs are different from ours; that *hippie* is a derogatory term often applied to anyone with long hair; and that far from being chiselers, eight out of ten welfare recipients are either too young, too old, or too ill to work. When we laugh without explaining, that confirms Archie's stereotype.

When a visitor uses a term involving a prejudice we don't want our children to acquire, we can live up to our role as primary educators by offsetting it with an explanation then and there. Suppose Mr. Jones speaks of an Okie. We can say to the listening children, "Okies are poor farmers who have to leave the farm to find another job." The chances are that the speaker will be disarmed. In any event, we shall have made our point with the children.

We are well aware when friends and relatives are expressing an unchristian attitude, yet we're frequently too timid to deal with it. We don't have to confront them, but we do need to offset their remarks if we are to remain faithful to our principles in our children's eyes. It's silly to teach them that it's wrong to discriminate and then expect them to watch us accepting blatant put-downs of others without a murmur.

4. We commit ourselves to facts and information instead of myths. This year how many people will die of starvation in our world? in our country? in our state? Do we know? Do we want to know? How many elderly live alone in substandard flats on insufficient incomes, waiting to be released by death? What is the average income of the suburban family? the Amerindian? the Appalachian? the Honduran?

An excellent booklet available from the Campaign for Human Development, *Poverty Profile*, supplies abundant facts and statistics in a way that is easily understood. From a definition of poverty to common myths about it, this study presents the scope of poverty as it is—not as we'd like to believe it to be. Many other aids for families and classes are available from the Campaign for Human Development, all at the same mailing address: 1312 Massachusetts Avenue, N.W., Washington, D.C. 20005. Send for a brochure.

Another source of information is the Institute of Social Relations, Archdiocese of Newark, 300 Broadway, Newark, NJ 07104. The Institute's simulation games with regard to hunger (in which the family undertakes for a stated period to reduce its food intake to that of the poor) will help our families not only to learn the facts about hunger but actually to feel the frustration of being poor and hungry.

And don't forget the public library with its wealth of reference material on current social problems.

5. We commit ourselves to action. Many of us made the above four commitments long ago, but we never got around to acting on them. One of the final steps in internalizing a value is acting on it repeatedly. Prior to that step, all other steps are considered merely value indicators, not values themselves. Talking about poverty and even publicly affirming a need to counter poverty conditions aren't enough.

If we're sincere about teaching Christian attitudes rather than cultural myths in our family, we have to *do* something about the needy. Depending on the ages of our children and the state of the family resources, we can institute a campaign for human development within our own family, not just to help others (though they will also benefit) but to develop our own humanity. I suggest that individual families consider some of the following undertakings:

- cutting meat consumption in half
- fasting one day a week
- shopping for clothing at a thrift shop
- collecting for UNICEF at Halloween instead of trick-or-treating

- celebrating an alternative-style Christmas
- setting aside a percentage of your income (children's as well as parents') for others
- matching luxury spending (everything we spend on unnecessary items we match in funds for others)
- adopting as a relation an elderly man or woman who has been abandoned to loneliness
- financially adopting a poor family
- getting to know those who are poor in other ways: living empty, unloved, hedonistic lives
- learning what causes the poverty cycle, particularly what causes people to live within it
- giving time to others if money is short
- getting to know the poor in your own area, family to family
- sending a poor child to camp along with your own
- becoming an outlet for poor people's crafts
- working within a church or other group to discover needs and alleviate suffering in your community
- boycotting products derived from the exploitation of workers
- working actively for political candidates who are dedicated to eradicating injustice
- attending fair-housing meetings and speaking up at them; writing letters to editors to expose myths about poverty; becoming courageous foes of poverty and injustice

These are but a few of the many positive things we can do if we are truly committed as a family to helping our neighbors. The Scriptures are concrete in their proposals about helping others, and sometimes our children have a better grasp of reality than we have. They don't rationalize away Matthew 25:44-45: " 'Lord, when did we see you hungry or thirsty, a stranger or naked, sick or in prison, and did not come to your help?' Then he will answer, 'I tell you solemnly, in so far as you neglected to do this to one of the least of these, you neglected to do it to me.' "

Our children just wonder why we don't do anything.

CHAPTER 12

Television—
Our Electronic Hearth?

Hearth is one of those words full of imagery. It conjures up warm thoughts of family, intimacy, and quiet sharing. Television has been called our new hearth, but the imagery it invokes is in direct contrast to hearth words: individual rather than family, escape rather than intimacy, and privacy rather than sharing.

When Eda LeShan, one of the best child psychologists around, was asked her opinion on the right of parents to monitor children's television, she replied, "We don't allow a five-year-old to see *Last Tango in Paris*. We don't allow our children to live exclusively on popcorn and soda. We carefully choose our child's pediatrician, neighborhood, and school. If it's snowing, the boots go on, no matter how loud the protests.

"We consider it a parental prerogative to do our best to keep our kids from getting run over in traffic or burning themselves on a hot stove. Why shouldn't we know what our children are exposed to when the set goes on?"

Why not indeed? It's obvious now that parents have to do the monitoring. The so-called Family Viewing Hour was doomed from the start. It was ridiculed to death. Sponsors, programmers, and actors collectively gathered forces to kill it. After *Born Innocent* was shown during the Family Hour and the loud outcries from parents were ignored by the industry, the subject of the Family Hour became a matter of jest for television.

TV homemaker Sue Ann on "The Mary Tyler Moore Show" asked, "How many things can you do with an egg—especially during the Family Hour?"

On "Phyllis," one character said to another, "Why don't we just go upstairs and play Scrabble until Family Hour is over?"

Sonny and Cher delivered at least one Family Hour joke per show, and the late-night talk shows actively encouraged guests to deride the Family Hour as something demanded by small-minded people.

Families didn't have a chance. We couldn't talk back. We didn't have equal air time. Finally, the Hour was found unconstitutional, and our helplessness over the repast of rapes, sadism, and murder served up to our children during prime time reached a peak.

Monitoring television has become one of the most frustrating responsibilities of parents. Media influence was the most pervasive, yet elusive, complaint in the Call to Action consultation, which drew responses from over 800,000 Catholics across the nation. Respondents mentioned it throughout the consultation, but few gave suggestions for handling it—a sure sign of helplessness and frustration.

Since one of the dividends of parenting in the television age is a responsibility for handling media images and attitudes, it's important that we become knowledgeable about the effects of media upon our children.

Educating Ourselves to the Impact of TV

Most parents are ignorant of the statistics surrounding television. When I tell parents that by the time their children graduate from high school, they will have spent 11,000 hours in school and 15,000 hours in front of television, or that by age fifteen the average child has viewed 13,000 violent deaths, most are appalled.

Here are a few more statistics to boggle your mind:
- Children spend more time watching TV than in any other activity except sleeping.
- Television leads all other traditional influences on

our lives. (Religion ranks twenty-third out of twenty-four.)

- In the average home, the TV set is on for forty-four hours a week.
- The University of Virginia recently reported that among three- to five-year-olds, eighty percent prefer Mommy to TV and only fifty-four percent prefer Daddy to TV.
- One thousand leaders of American Life, asked to name the most powerful institutions in America, listed these top three: The White House, the Supreme Court, and television.
- The average male viewer, between his second and sixty-fifth year, will watch television for over 3,000 entire days or roughly nine full years of his life.
- The Surgeon General's 1972 report on television violence cited nearly fifty studies which conclude that the more violence a youngster sees on TV, the more aggressive he or she is likely to become in attitude and action.
- By the time the average child enters kindergarten he or she has already spent more hours learning about the world from television than the hours one would spend in a college classroom earning a B.A. degree.

These statistics clearly point out the primacy of television's influence, yet we seem content to remain ignorant of its potential, its impact, and our power over it. Perhaps we think that by complaining to one another we've done all we can do.

Who is responsible for educating parents about television, about how to use it and how to control it? The public schools? The Church? The industry itself? I prefer to think that all three, as leading institutions in our lives, have a stake in it, but in the absence of any positive effort being offered, I suggest that the Church take it on. Workshops, lectures, and courses on television and the family are a must for an electronic generation. There are excellent books out to educate all of us about the media. Any one of the following would serve as a fine text for a parish or diocesan course on the home and the media. I found most of the books in my own public library, but I like the first one so well I bought my own copy.

The Family Guide to Children's Television—What to Watch, What to Miss, What to Change and How to Do It by Evelyn Kaye, Pantheon Books.

Television and Society by Harry J. Skornia, McGraw-Hill paperbacks.

What's on Tonight? by James Brieg, Ligouri Publications.

How to Talk Back to Your Television Set by Nicholas Johnson, Little, Brown and Company.

Television and Growing Up: The Impact of Televised Violence, report to the Surgeon General, U.S. Government Printing Office.

Television in the Lives of Our Children by Schramm, Lyle, and Parker, Stanford University Press.

The Incredible Television Machine by Lee Polk and Eda LeShan, Macmillan Publishing Company.

TV, the Anonymous Teacher, a fifteen-minute color film, Mass Media Ministries.

Facing up to What Television Replaces

It isn't normal for children to sit motionless for three hours. Their minds may be captured, but their muscles and imaginations are stifled. Parents simply have to turn off the set and say, "Go outside and run." Play and creativity can be minimized in the child—or adult—who is willing to sink into the set day after day. This produces the kind of zombie for whom other activities become "too much work."

I interviewed a significant number of kindergarten teachers the year after "Sesame Street" exploded on the pre-school scene. I was writing an article on the effects of the program on youngsters, and I asked teachers if there was a noticeable difference between the kindergartners who had seen a year of "Sesame Street" and their pre-Sesame counterparts. Most of the teachers mentioned two emerging traits: a need for constant variety and change ("On 'Sesame Street' the alphabet is faster," explained one tot) and a reluctance to participate in class activity. The "Sesametized" youngsters preferred watching over doing—a first step toward that passivity that so frustrates parents and teachers today.

Almost all teachers point to increased student resistance to routine learning such as spelling, math tables, and other basic memory skills. "It's boring" is the usual excuse students give when their skill failure is pointed out, as if that were a legitimate reason for refusing to learn.

Yet, repetition is necessary in order to learn personal skills. One simply isn't going to learn to write by watching even the most delightful cartoon on how to write. Spelling requires concentration and rote memory work, as do multiplication tables, typing exercises, and chemistry symbols. Dr. Calvin Anderson of the Colorado Department of Education pointed to television as a factor discouraging children from sticking to a task because "It edits out the dullness of practice, all of the routine necessary to achieve excellence."

In many families, communication has broken down completely. It becomes a sad cycle: families can't talk together because the TV is on, so they forget how to talk together, so they watch television—even at meals—so they don't have to talk together. We're faced with the irony of having the greatest variety of ideas ever available to a family gathered together and the least opportunity to share them. "Shhh" and "Move" are two common responses to any attempt to elaborate on ideas. We wait for the commercial and then forget what we intended to say.

The heavy-viewing family begins to eliminate other activities one by one. First it's the little walks, picnics, and visits that go. After that it's entertaining others, ice skating, and days at the beach. All become too much work when there's a set that can be sunk into collectively at will. What this costs in terms of family intimacy is staggering. Many children of two-parent, moderate-means families share no leisure time activities with their parents outside of television and vacations. Paradoxically, many heavy-viewing families relish vacations that take them "away from it all"—camping, fishing, mountains—because in reality, in the absence of the demanding family autocrat, the TV set, these vacations are bringing them back to one another.

Eventually a resentment toward anything that intrudes upon television surfaces in the heavy-viewing family. "We can't come Monday night because there's football, Tuesday because..." is a common plaint from parents heard by teachers and preachers. Even more common is the child's wail upon hearing of a Scouting function or a proposed visit from relatives: "But that's when 'Gilligan's Island' is on!"

It seems vital that families periodically review their leisure-time habits. Do they consider other activities when they have free time, or do they automatically depend upon TV? If Mom doesn't say, "Let's go on a hike," is that it? Is the family placing the burden of shared activity upon her? Is the family gradually becoming a heavy-viewing family although it considers itself a light-viewing family? How many leisure activities outside of television did the family share in the past three months? Are meals planned around television? Does the family reject invitations because of favorite shows? Does the family feel it necessary to tote along a portable set when camping or otherwise away from television?

Using Television to Enrich Family Life

One of television's most exciting offerings was its 1977 series on *Roots*. The show had many intrinsic values ranging from educating us on the lived experiences of slaves to explaining present attitudes of and toward Blacks in America. But one unsung bonus was the bonding of families who watched the show together. It was the first time that many families sat together and watched a series, and parents commented on that experience:

"Our family talks about it at every meal. We sure hope there's a sequel."

"My teenage son wants to get the book and find out how Alex Haley traced the story. I hope he does because we'd like to know more about it, too."

"I was surprised that our teenagers wanted to watch *Roots* instead of *Helter Skelter* (the Charles Manson story which played opposite *Roots* in many parts of the country). After every segment, they stuck around to talk about it."

"As a family, we really learned about slavery together. Now we all want to know more about it."

Note the number of times parents mentioned the increased interest in the subject matter aroused by *Roots*. I'm convinced that part of the interest lay in the mutuality of parents and children viewing it together. The series was on an adult level, not the usual seventh-grade level of most shows, and as such it often demanded that parents lead their children into an understanding of what was being dramatized.

Roots had a strong impact on our family. Our two oldest, then eleven and fifteen, had many questions. We made the decision early in the series not to duck discussion of the more brutal parts.

When Kunte Kinte's toe was cut off after his second attempt to run away, our daughter was indignant. "How could they do that to him?" she raged.

"They owned him," we replied. "They felt they had a right to do anything they wanted to him."

"But that's horrible," she said. "How could people let that happen?"

"It was slavery. Slaves were considered property. People paid a lot of money for them and felt that entitled them to treat their slaves like property."

"But that didn't make it right," she insisted. "Why didn't some of the good people stop it?"

"They did," replied her dad. "They called it the Civil War."

I think it was the first time she really understood the emotion that led our country into that war.

On another episode our son was confused about the use and abuse of the black woman's body by the foreman. We explained that the slave owners and foremen felt they had a right to sleep with the slave woman because they owned her.

"That's not fair," he said. "I mean if they owned her, I can see how they felt they had a right to make her work. But, gee, your body is your own. I mean, if your body isn't your own, what is?"

The concepts that *Roots* demonstrated were a bit difficult for children used to the non-demanding scripts of "Happy Days," but their difficulty actually enhanced appreciation once they were explained.

We can use television in this way more often. Public television, particularly, offers outstanding series on great drama, National Geographic specials, documentaries, great moments and movements in history, transportation, and famous battles. But some families never turn to public or educational television other than to watch "Sesame Street."

I don't want to give the impression that public television has the only worthwhile programs. Increasingly, the major networks are sponsoring good drama and specials. The value to the family lies in being selective and in viewing together. Eda LeShan, the psychologist I quoted earlier, commends viewing together as a family. "Watching television together gives parents an opportunity to find out what their children are thinking and feeling," she says, "as well as providing an opportunity for parents to communicate their values to help shape children's attitudes."

Surely none of us wants to watch TV with our children all the time, but when we are aware of an unusually good offering, we can make it a point to watch with them. At times I insist that the children watch a special like *Huckleberry Finn* instead of a rerun of "Hogan's Heroes" simply because I know it's a better program. (I also insist occasionally that they read a book instead of a comic book.) Although they argue a bit at first, they usually like the better program.

A second method of enriching family life through the tube is to obtain and read the books upon which favorite shows were based. Many parents who would never have otherwise read *Charlotte's Web* or the Pooh stories aloud with their children did so after viewing those specials. This is a real potential of television: whetting appetites for more. Publishers know that millions of books are sold after a series is offered. *Upstairs Downstairs, Captains and Kings, Rich Man, Poor Man, Mash, Helter Skelter,* and hundreds of other books hit the top of the best-seller lists immediately after the TV series.

We don't have to limit ourselves to the actual book itself, either. As with *Roots*, we wanted to know more about slavery, not as a political issue but as it affected people then. A wise parent will search out other books on the subject to take advantage of the interest instilled by television. Teachers have bibliographies and actual copies of books ready for students who want to know more. TV's greatest value today could be the way it instills a desire to read and learn more.

Another method overlooked by parents in using television in the family is to use programs with rotten values to teach good values. We always need good horrible examples, and they abound in many of the police and talk shows and soap operas. Too often, parents allow immoral behavior, cruelty to lessers, and hedonism to slip by on the screen without comment. As the Surgeon General's report indicates, parents' verbalized attitudes toward such values are prime influences on the child's attitudes.

When we're watching "Hogan's Heroes," for example, and realize the Nazi officers are being portrayed as loveable old gents, we can point out that these were the men responsible for the death of six million Jews and others. When we did that in our own family, our adolescent, who was outraged at Hitler's treatment of the Jews because she was reading *The Diary of a Young Girl* by Anne Frank and *The Hiding Place*, admitted she had never thought about it that way before. We need to offer that kind of balance.

When heroes are obviously sleeping around, we can wonder aloud why they're portrayed as heroes when they have so little respect for themselves and others. The message gets across. We don't have to preach, but neither do we have to keep our judgment to ourselves. If one of our children's friends was sitting there expounding the same values and behavior, we'd surely offset it with our remarks, maybe even banish him or her from our children's circle of friends. Why are we so reluctant to criticize the prime influencer?

Occasionally it's a good technique for parents and children to watch a particular show like "One Day at a Time," which deals with some fairly realistic family situations, and then turn off the set and talk about it. We did this after the four-part series on "One Day at a Time" when Julie ran away with her boy friend. Should her mother have begged her to come back on her own terms? "No," replied our children soundly, but they pointed out that Julie's mother had driven her away by forbidding her to see the boy friend. It was a worthwhile discussion and one that gave all of us insights into how the others felt about running away and about its causes and remedies.

Viewing together can help develop our children's taste in TV, too. Just as in reading, the better the shows they view, the better the shows they will demand. Our own children now find some programs that they previously enjoyed silly, and they switch channels to find something better or turn to some other activity. When we first began watching *Upstairs Downstairs*, which was on our educational channel, our oldest happened to watch with us. She was hooked into it immediately and made a comment to the effect that she didn't know there was anything that good on educational TV. Now all of our children scan that channel's offerings along with the others.

Not in wide use yet, but surely a prime way of using television to help families, is the coming videodisc system. According to Father Anthony Scannell, O.F.M., within five years the majority of American families will have videodisc systems attached to their television sets. These systems will enable them to view programs of their own choosing at any time they wish. His Franciscan Communications Center in Los Angeles is already producing "Storyscape" religious programs for these discs.

"The new low-cost audio-visual medium for the home opens a whole new area for religious education centered around the family," Father Anthony explained. The videodiscs will look like phonograph records and will be played on a special turntable attached easily to the TV set. "We have in mind a series of thirty programs built around the sacraments and geared to family religious education," he said.

Finally, parents can use television to their advantage when children are sick, need companionship, or are under too much pressure and need to sink into escape. Television was, and still is, essentially an entertainment medium, although it's gradually becoming more than that. There are times when children need to escape into such entertainment. When a child is pressured to over-achieve or to meet someone else's expectations, an entertaining and undemanding TV show can relieve the tension for awhile. When parents aren't home from work and friends are busy, TV helps a lonely time pass more quickly. To sum up, TV has the potential to help or to harm.

Who Owns the Knob?

One of the imperatives of good family viewing is establishment of standards, quantity, and quality of programs. Many families allow unlimited, unmonitored viewing. While this may be costly in fomenting negative values, passivity, and lack of creativity, its highest price might be its denying the children the chance to be selective. Who appreciates candy more, the child who is allowed free rein in the candy store, or the one who is allowed to spend a quarter there once in awhile?

One method found to be successful in many families is to limit television viewing to an hour or two daily, leaving it up to the individual child to select the times he or she wishes to view. An obvious drawback is the parental bookkeeping required. I'm sure my children would take advantage of my forgetfulness to poach on another's programs. But this control does force children to be more selective. If they can watch only one hour, they aren't going to waste it on a thirty-first rerun of "Gilligan's Island" but will save it for "Good Times" or "Bob Newhart."

Other families permit unlimited viewing once homework and chores are finished satisfactorily. We've used a variety of methods in our family, settling into a general rule that certain programs aren't allowed—"Starsky and Hutch," for instance because of the violence—and that the set doesn't go on until after dinner. We aren't a heavy-viewing family. The set doesn't go on with the coffee pot in the morning. Unless there's something special like the Inauguration, it isn't on at all during the day.

When we allowed TV watching after school, we found that the younger children weren't out getting exercise and that they even resented taking time out for dinner chores. Eliminating it after school was a good move for us. Now they automatically grab a football and run outside, or if the weather is bad, they play inside together—a necessary opportunity for socializing that many children are not forced to have today.

They also appreciate their evening viewing more. For our nine-year-old that amounts to about an hour a day and for our twelve-year-old about two. Our teenager is too busy to watch much TV. We allow her unlimited viewing as long as she doesn't misuse it, but we still censor certain programs for her.

Regulating TV doesn't have to be a constant struggle, but it does require a constant awareness. The parents who have the most difficulty monitoring their children's television are usually those who are most addicted themselves. It's hard to tell a child to run outside and play if the parent watches all day long. A recent *Redbook* magazine study showed what happened when a group of parents put their children on a TV "diet"—limiting them to an hour a day. At first, the children showed symptoms similar to those of an adult quitting smoking: increased irritableness and restlessness. Once past that stage, however, they calmed down and showed improvement in manners, attention span, and homework. So perseverance on the part of parents in limiting TV is important.

Joining Support Groups

Parents have some power in controlling TV, not only in their homes but on the airwaves. Here are names and addresses of some organizations and newsletters dedicated to promoting better television. You can write for more information. I am also listing the addresses of the networks themselves so that you can write to protest or to praise, and the address of the FCC, where you can send copies of the letters you have sent to the networks.

Action for Children's Television (ACT) is probably the best-known organization designed to improve what our children are viewing. One of ACT's goals is to educate parents on the uses and abuses of the medium. "Broadcasters have told us that for every letter they get—criticism or praise—they assume there are a hundred other people who feel the same way who have not written," according to an ACT spokeswoman. "Letters do make an impression." *ACT Quarterly* (newsletter); 46 Austin St., Newtonville, MA 02160.

Project Focus Newsletter, edited by Shirley A. Lieberman, clarifies the role, place, and impact of television in our lives. *Viewsletter* is published monthly September through June and includes articles, addresses, and some program reviews. $3.25 a year. For sample copy write 1061 Brook Ave., St. Paul, MN 55113.

Better Radio and Television, P.O. Box 43640, Los Angeles, CA 90043.

National Association for Better Broadcasting, 373 N. Western Avenue, Los Angeles, CA 90004. An excellent quarterly; $4.00 a year.

National Citizen's Committee for Broadcasting, 1028 Connecticut Avenue, Washington, D.C. 21136. They periodically publish lists of the most violent and least violent programs and the sponsors of these programs.

ABC Television Network, 1330 Avenue of the Americas, New York, NY 10019.

CBS Television Network, 51 West 52nd St., New York, NY 10019.

NBC Television Network, 50 Rockefeller Plaza, New York, NY 10020.

Federal Communications Commission (FCC), 1919 M Street, NW, Washington, D.C. 20054.

Public Broadcasting Service, 475 L'Enfant Plaza West, SW, Washington, D.C. 20024.

Everglades Publishing Company, P.O. Drawer Q, Everglades, FL 33929; publishes TV sponsors' directory.

Television Awareness Training (TAT) is an adult study about television and visual literacy. Leadership training and materials are available from *Media Action Research Center,* 474 Riverside Drive, Suite 1370, New York, NY 10027.

CHAPTER 13

What's Ahead for the Family?

By now readers are probably feeling a bit overwhelmed at
the variety of subjects I've included in a book for Catholic
parents, especially if they were expecting new motivation
and methods for teaching the Commandments and found
instead television, sexuality, and moral development.

They will empathize with the Air Force chaplain who
asked me to come and motivate the parents, "to get them
moving to do something in their families." I accepted his
charge and, with a bit more enthusiasm than usual, I
encouraged listening parents, "Ask your chaplain for some
help on understanding moral development," and "Your
pastor will be happy to supply you with books and films
on sexuality education," and "Your chaplain is waiting for
you to ask him for help on family celebration," and the
like.

Apparently I overdid it, because the following day a
depressed chaplain drove me to the airport. After moments
of leaden silence, he turned to me and asked despairingly,
"What am I supposed to do now? They're already asking
me for help in all those areas, and I don't know where to
start."

I checked a laugh. It was such a parental kind of
reaction—wanting the children to get excited and active in
religion without demanding much of the parent. I presume
he rose to his flock's expectations, though, because I heard
from several parishioners later that interesting projects

were going on in their parish. But I'm more careful now not to enthuse parents beyond the pastor's expectations and limitations.

"Where do I start?" is a predictable question in parishes today. Swirling about us are appalling predications on the future of the family. Is the family as we know it going to disappear? Are we dealing with the real needs, or only with the symptoms? And what do parents want, anyway?

For the first time in the history of our Church, we have an idea of what parents want from their Church. We finally asked them, and over 800,000 of them shared not only the issues about *Family* that they would like to see the Church address but also the actions to take to meet those issues.

This process was part of the American Bishops' bicentennial Call to Action consultation in 1976. I was privileged to serve on the writing committee on *Family*, so I was in on the consultation from the beginning. Material gathered from nine national hearings, dozens of diocesan hearings, hundreds of parish discussion groups, and thousands of individual feedback sheets was fed into the computer. The printout was sent to writers to draft into recommendations upon which diocesan delegates voted the following October.

For some months, *Family* led significantly in the number of issues submitted from around the country. It ultimately ended up second to *Church*. Perhaps respondents were telling us that until their needs are met in the community closest to them, the family, they cannot get deeply involved in solving the problems of others.

Interestingly, the same issues that first rose to the top of the list stayed there throughout the consultation. I believe our first printout reached us in March and represented only 30,000 issues and actions. Eventually the consultation counted 825,000 responses, but the same top issues held. They changed positions slightly in succeeding printouts, but they held steadily as the top eight, regardless of diocese of origin.

Responses from laity in the so-called "conservative" dioceses and "liberal" dioceses were remarkably similar. From this we may presume that family needs and desires across the country are pretty much the same and that diocesan ideology doesn't seem to influence the needs—although diocesan response and lack of response to those needs does have an impact.

What did the American Catholic family ask of its Church?

1. Support for family values topped the list. Over 70,000 respondents asked for reinforcement on the value of the family in today's society, help in teaching values, respect, dignity and self image, more family prayer and worship activities like the home Mass, and help in promoting cultural and religious traditions in the home.

2. Family-life education was a close second. This included all kinds of parish educational programs: parenting skills, realistic premarriage, marriage, and divorce education, sexuality education for both children and parents, and assistance in dealing with the aged, the handicapped, and other special family people.

3. Divorce came next. It included a myriad of issues facing the divorced Catholic in our Church and specifically asked for a change in attitude toward the divorced in our parishes. Many respondents who were divorced stated that they no longer felt welcome or at home in our Church. They also asked for a parish and diocesan focus on the spiritual and social needs of the divorced.

4. Communication skills followed. Catholics asked their . Church to help them communicate better with one anothei, their Church, and their school. A particular mention was made of husband-wife and parent-teenager communication.

When I did a column on this list asking readers to rate the issues and send them to me, they placed communication skills first. If I were in a parish leadership position, either as pastor, DRE, or a council member, I would press for immediate courses, lectures, workshops, discussions, books, and lessons on marriage and family communication. I believe some of the most successful grassroots programs in our Church such as Marriage Encounter, Parent Effectiveness Training, and the charismatic movement are popular because they offer training in communication skills not offered elsewhere.

5. Pressures against family life came next. Catholic parents asked for help in offsetting values contrary to Christian life promoted by television and movies and for help in dealing with issues that have an influence on family life: the new permissiveness, drugs, alcohol, advertising, mobility, music, affluence, unemployment, the women's movement.

6. Counseling came next, with thousands of laity asking the Church for professional marriage, family, and teenage counseling.

7. Family sense of vocation/social witness told us that parents are seeking help in developing a sense of compassion in the family. They want to learn how to be a family that reaches out to help others in our often-impersonal society. They asked for a family-to-family ministry program.

8. Single parents completed the list of the top eight issues. Single Catholic parents (and their families) asked for help with parenting, overcoming loneliness, empty spirituality, a sense of unworthiness, and guilt. They also wanted help from their Church in supplying missing-parent role models— the "share a Dad/Mom" idea found in some churches.

When the delegates met in Detroit, they had studied the issues, actions, and working resolutions that we on the writing committees had offered. They discussed, amended, and rewrote many of them. Ultimately they passed the

following resolutions, which were then turned over to the
bishops for consideration.   ❧

Recommendations:

Support for Family Values   Christ, our Savior, spoke both
beautifully and forcefully of the permanence and
indissolubility of marriage. In response to his teaching and
to assist the whole Catholic community to reaffirm its
support of the beauty, dignity, and sacramentality of
marriage and the family and to increase its awareness that
Christian marriage is meant to be a great sign of Christ's
love for the Church, we recommend:

1. That this assembly affirm: a) that committed, life-long
marriage is part of God's plan; b) that when husbands and
wives love each other, they serve God; c) that children are
an expression of the creative fruitfulness of human life and
love; d) that to live in peace and security is the right and
duty of every family, beginning in service to its members;
e) that each family, as one among many families in the
world, finds fulfillment in service to others; f) that within
the common bonds of faith, each family has the right, and
is encouraged to express its religious values within the
context of its cultural heritage and to share it with others; g)
that within the Christian family commitment marriage and
family life should also enhance the freedom of men and
women to fulfill their personal potential and participate
fully in the life of their world; and h) that there is a
powerful witness in loving families in which parents have
been separated by divorce, death, or economic crisis and in
which a single parent and children cooperate in nurturing
and supporting one another.

2. That the whole Church, through the example of the
lives of its members and through action undertaken in
cooperation with other religious and civic groups, pledges
itself to combat those contemporary social, economic, and
cultural forces which threaten all families.

There is a special need within the Church for theologians to collaborate in developing further the theology of matrimony. Recognizing the special needs of married couples and families, we strongly believe that a catechesis of marriage, sexuality, and family based on contemporary and sound theology and the lived experience of the married should be implemented on every level of the Church's life. This educational process should involve the Church in educational programs for effective parenthood. This catechesis should create a favorable impression of marriage and an appropriate understanding of sexuality.

3. That the Church, with the leadership of the bishops, develop a comprehensive pastoral plan for family ministry based upon a continuing process of dialogue between families and competent authorities.

Recognizing the value of the traditional nuclear family, we see a need to broaden our concept and practice of family ministry to families of diverse lifestyles, including, but not limited to, single-parent families, childless couples, widowed and separated people.

In developing such a plan, particular concern should be shown for:

a. The racial, ethnic, and cultural diversity of the Catholic community;

b. The need for family-centered worship and religious education, both in the home and in the parish; we further recommend that Sunday be truly the Lord's day by establishing the day as a family day for all the members of the parish. In addition to the liturgy, the day shall include educational, recreational, and paraliturgical celebrations;

c. Pastoral programs which encourage formation of family groups for prayer, worship, sacramental preparation, marriage enrichment, family life education, and mutual support, either within parishes or across parish boundaries;

d. The need for consideration of the family in Catholic programs of social service at all levels;

e. The need to develop an overall vision of social

legislation that will strengthen marriage and foster family life, including legislation to protect the rights of parents to the moral guidance of their children;

f. The need to utilize the resources of other private and public agencies in the community if the needs of all families are to be served;

g. The need to formulate diocesan policies that would not only stress marriage as a sacramental vocation within the Church but also apply some of the same safeguards and principles of preparation utilized in readying candidates for Holy Orders;

h. The need for providing information, counseling, and support for families who have members who are part of a "sexual minority";

i. We further recommend that the bishops declare in the near future a family year.

4. That the bishops in conjunction with existing Catholic marriage and family life movements provide a national structure to formulate and implement a pastoral plan for integrated family ministry. This structure should involve:

a. Establishment of a standing committee of the National Conference of Catholic Bishops with responsibility for marriage and family life. Furthermore, we strongly recommend the enlargement and support of the National Family Life Office by July 1, 1977;

b. Prompt establishment and support for diocesan family life offices with appropriate diocesan, vicariate, deanery, and parish committees. To further this goal, we urge that every diocese name at least a family life liaison officer by September 1, 1977;

c. Recognition of the special competency of permanent deacons and lay people, especially married couples, in family ministry by seeking them out and assuring them roles of leadership and authority;

d. Appropriate training for all those involved in leadership positions in family ministry;

e. A just allocation of Church resources, on every level, for family ministry programs and a review of all present church budgets in order to bring about an equitable distribution of personnel and finances for supporting these programs.

Family and Society   In order to assist the Catholic family to fulfill its responsibility to assist other families and participate in the redemption and transformation of society through an awareness of the constitutive gospel dimension of action on behalf of social justice, we recommend:

1. That all programs dealing in family life, at all levels in the Church, address in a special way the specific education of families in making them aware of the needs of others in their neighborhood, their local communities, or in the world community. These family life efforts will work with other social justice agencies to create environments and develop programs which encourage families to get involved in an action and reflection process in the service of others and the attainment of justice.

2. That ministry to strong marriages, as well as those in difficulty, be recognized as part of the social justice dimension of family life and that organizations and movements which specialize in marriage and family life include and/or develop programs dealing with the social justice dimension of family life and provide materials, models, resources, and skills to enable families to open themselves to the injustices in the world, to reach out to those in need, and to provide channels through which they can contribute to the solution of such problems of injustice.

3. That the entire Catholic community regularly and systematically participate in developing a clear position on public policy and legislation. This public policy and legislation most specifically should promote societal conditions based on human rights and social justice which allow all families and individuals to function as free human beings. Further, public policy and legislation should protect the rights of families to participate in decision making regarding, but not limited to, education, total health care, and moral guidance of their members.

In order to help families arrive at positions of personal involvement and organized political action, the National Conference of Catholic Bishops and each diocese should work out mechanisms for organizing families into coalitions on family-related issues. To achieve these ends, we recommend the establishment of pastoral councils on the national, regional, diocesan, district, parish, and neighborhood levels. State Catholic Conferences and the United States Catholic Conference, in implementing programs for political responsibility and social action, should consult with these councils and give priority attention to developing positions on issues of public policy which affect family life. Where possible, there should be ecumenical participation.

4. That families, as part of a pastoral social justice program related to media, and aided by parish and diocesan family life commissions, in cooperation with diocesan communications offices, the United States Catholic Conference Department of Communication, UNDA-USA (Catholic Association of Broadcasters and allied communicators) and the Catholic Press Association and other religious and civic organizations and coalitions:
—Initiate or support efforts to *evaluate* the impact on family life of present and developing social communication media;
—And suggest positive actions for family utilization of and involvement in media.

That families, especially with the structures mentioned above and other organizations and coalitions dedicated to better broadcasting:
—Work to *promote* the human and aesthetic quality of network and local programming and policies in order to counteract dehumanizing values of consumerism and materialism;
—Work for the further limitation of programming depicting excessive violence and irresponsible sex:

a) through government regulatory agencies;
b) through local station accountability and ascertainment procedures;
c) through influencing program sponsors.

That families work again through the above mentioned structures to *support* programming which reinforces family values.

The Church and Divorced Catholics   We pledge ourselves to a serious effort to reconcile separated and divorced and remarried Catholics within our community of faith. Toward that end we recommend:

1. That dioceses and parishes extend pastoral care to separated, divorced, and divorced/remarried Catholics by the development and implementation of effective programs of ministry, education, and group support.

2. That the people of God in the local Catholic communities put an immediate end to practices which brand separated, divorced, and divorced/remarried Catholics as failures or discriminate against them or their children in parish or diocesan activities; further, that educational programs be developed and funded aimed at eliminating discriminatory attitudes which underlie these practices.

3. That the Church leaders publicly address the request of the divorced who have remarried to receive, under certain conditions, the sacraments of the Church. We ask this because many Catholic people do not understand that many divorced who have remarried are not necessarily excluded from the eucharist. We ask the bishops to develop more consistent, equitable, effective, and more pastorally oriented procedures for dealing with annulment and dissolution of marriages throughout all the dioceses of the United States of America.

4. That the Church invest in serious study of the causes of marital breakdown with particular attention to the impact of cultural conditions on marriage and family life. These studies, conducted in dialogue with married as well as separated, divorced, and divorced/remarried Catholics, would help shape realistic policies for strengthening family life.

5. That the bishops of the United States take the action required to repeal the penalty of automatic excommunication decreed by the Third Council of Baltimore for Catholics who "dare to remarry after divorce."

While I realize that these recommendations are broad, they certainly can be used by parishes and parents working together to enrich family life. Some of the resolutions require a change in Church law. We can do nothing about those until the bishops act, but the majority of actions can be met in the parish without great cost or controversy.

I would like to see a parish evaluate its attitude toward the divorced, for example. Does it unintentionally give the impression that the divorced are unwelcome simply because the plethora of organizations and activities are dedicated to the two-parent family? Has the parish ever offered anything for the divorced and their needs? for the widowed? for the single parent? for the childless? for the never-married? Or is it run like Noah's ark, everything by twos?

As for the family itself, what are its responsibilities in nudging its parish into action? Readers can ask parish councils and parish leaders to consider some of the needs mentioned in the consultation which aren't being addressed in their parish. The family is the beneficiary of such action, after all, and should be part of the initiation, implementation, and evaluation processes.

Take for example an average parish that hasn't scrutinized its organizations or goals much in the past ten years. A couple sincerely dedicated to the idea of bolstering today's family through the Church could approach the parish council and ask them to read the first recommendation, "Support for Family Values," with an eye toward evaluating present parish efforts.

Perhaps the parish could devote a whole year to showing concern for *"Pastoral programs which encourage formation of family groups for prayer, worship, sacramental preparation, marriage enrichment, family life education, and mutual support, either within parishes or across parish boundaries."*

Parishioners could be invited to suggest ways in which these goals could be met. Could they share a marriage counselor or a marriage enrichment weekend with a couple of other parishes? What is the best way of forming family groups for prayer and worship in their particular parish? What do they want in the line of family-life education?—help in becoming sex educators, or classes for their children?

If we're a maturing laity, we can't lay the responsibility for the Catholic family on the bishops. They have a whole Church to care for, not just families. They expect us to take the initiative in seeking and meeting the needs of today's families, particularly now that we know what those needs are.

Cardinal John Dearden, in his opening address to the Call to Action conference said, "Throughout America, wherever Catholics were asked, they expressed their desire to share responsibility for the Church and the nation. They like parish and diocesan pastoral councils; they criticize their shortcomings, but they want these new structures. They want to work closely with their priests and bishops, and they want their leaders to trust them and be accountable to them for the use of Church resources."

Yes, we want our leaders to trust us and to be accountable to us. Likewise, we want to be trusted and to be accountable to them, to ourselves, to our brothers and sisters.

I have great hope for the family. It's being buffeted by new and sometimes frightening social forces, to be sure, but the family is resilient. It weathers crises such as unemployment, unplanned pregnancies, and unfulfilled dreams like no other institution does.

In this way, the family has much to teach the Church. While headlines become increasingly pessimistic over the future of the family, the family hangs right in there coping, working, and dreaming together.

In the beginning, there were the parents—and there still are.